AI Boosted Agile

Intelligent Agility: Flexing Mind from Revolution to Innovation

Ramakrishna Rao Tadepalli

Rajiv Banerjee

Suchinhita

ARCCHIE

AI Boosted Agile

Intelligent Agility: Flexing Mind from Revolution to Innovation

Editor: Gaurav Mutreja
Production Manager: Meghna and Alex
Cover design by Freepik and Vecteezy

First Edition: Dec-2024
Reference: 2411155
Published by Arcchie Publications
ISBN-13 (paperback): 978-81-979768-5-8
ISBN-13 (eBook): 978-81-979768-4-1

www.arcchieonline.com

DEDICATED TO

Honour thy Mother as God.
Honour thy Father as God.
Honour thy Teacher as God.
Honour thy Guest as God.
(**Taittiriya Upanishad**)
In the loving memory of my dear Father and Mother, Tadepalli Sankara Rao,
and Venkateswaramma, who have gracefully merged with divinity.
Their enduring presence continues to inspire and guide me.
- *Rama Tadepalli*

In the loving memory of my father, Samir Banerjee, who has journeyed beyond this life, yet his impact on me will never fade. My mother, Bani Banerjee, my wife, Jayati Banerjee, and my two children, Rohana and Rimon, provide me with the unwavering support to stay strong, positive, and forward-looking in this continuous journey of life.
- *Rajiv Banerjee*

I dedicate this book to my parents, Srijay & Rina Sengupta, my spouse, Sarmila Thakur, my daughter, Shriya Sengupta, and to all my family members and friends, who have always been my eternal source of inspiration.
- *Suchinhita*

ACKNOWLEDGMENT

This book results from countless insights, inspirations, and contributions from diverse individuals and sources of wisdom. We extend our heartfelt gratitude to everyone who has been a part of this transformative journey. We express our most profound appreciation to the community of AI enthusiasts, Agile practitioners, and product visionaries who continuously strive for excellence. Your relentless pursuit of innovation and ability to push the boundaries of what is possible has been our constant motivation. Your dedication to continuous improvement and change embodies the very spirit that this book seeks to celebrate and amplify. We offer our sincere thanks to the leaders who have shared their insights, experiences, and unwavering support. Your guidance and encouragement have been invaluable in shaping the ideas and frameworks presented in this book. Your vision and leadership continue to inspire teams and organizations to evolve and adapt in a rapidly changing world. We also pay our deepest respects to Sanatana Dharma and its revered Gurus. The eternal wisdom and spiritual guidance of this timeless tradition have illuminated our paths, providing us with clarity and purpose. Their teachings remind us of the importance of harmony, mindfulness, and the interconnectedness of all things—principles that resonate deeply with the ethos of Agile and AI.

Nature, the ultimate source of inspiration and change, holds a special place in our hearts. Its boundless beauty and intricate wisdom profoundly remind us of the importance of balance, adaptability, and sustainability. As we continue to innovate and transform, let us commit to preserving our planet for future generations, drawing lessons from nature's resilience and adaptability. Finally, we thank everyone who has supported us along this journey—our families, friends, colleagues, and readers. Your belief in our vision and encouragement have been the driving force behind this endeavor. Thank you for making this book possible and being part of our transformation journey. With heartfelt gratitude and boundless love, we dedicate this work to you.

- Rama Tadepalli, Rajiv Banerjee & Suchinhita

ABOUT THE AUTHORS

Rama Krishna Tadepalli is an experienced Transformation Leader with over 23 years of expertise in business analysis, program management, delivery execution, and organizational transformation. Rama, a passionate Gen-AI enthusiast, has successfully led Agile, product, and people-centric transformations for global clients. His hands-on leadership has supported teams ranging from hundreds to thousands, delivering multi-million-dollar outcomes while fostering long-term client and team satisfaction. Rama's expertise lies in designing and implementing innovative frameworks for executive coaching, leadership development, and change management. He has mentored over 500 leaders in emotional intelligence and servant leadership, blending real-world leadership insights with life coaching, spirituality, and a focus on aligning people with their purpose. Throughout his career, he has led successful transformations in 10 countries, coached over 200 mid-level managers through career transitions, and rescued numerous troubled projects through strategic leadership. Rama has also contributed to the field through his research, publishing a paper on "Backlog Health Assessment using Artificial Intelligence." An accomplished author of globally recognized books such as Agile Alchemy and Agile Odyssey, Rama continues to share his insights on transformation and leadership. As a dynamic public speaker and coach, he is passionate about fostering holistic growth and aligning purpose and value to achieve extraordinary outcomes. Rama invites connections to amplify success journeys and unlock the full potential of teams and leaders.

ABOUT THE AUTHORS

Rajiv Banerjee is a pioneer in Agile coaching and leadership, bringing over 20 years of IT experience in driving large-scale transformations and delivering outstanding results using frameworks like Scrum, SAFe, and Kanban. Rajiv has built a reputation as a committed Agile coaching and leadership professional. Specializing in frameworks such as Scrum, Kanban, SAFe, and XP, he currently leads large-scale Agile transformations. His expertise centers on empowering teams, fostering a culture of continuous improvement, and driving meaningful change within organizations. Rajiv has also made significant contributions to the field through his research, publishing two papers—one on "Team Health Assessment Using Artificial Intelligence" and the other on "Backlog Health Assessment Using Artificial Intelligence." An avid learner and connector, Rajiv welcomes opportunities to engage with others and explore new frontiers in technology and Agile practices.

Suchinhita, with nearly two decades of experience in the Information Technology industry, is an

avid advocate of Agile practices. Over the past decade, he has dedicated himself exclusively to roles within the Agile domain, including Agile Coach, Scrum Master, and Trainer. In addition, he is an aspiring Life Coach. As a co-author of the globally acclaimed books Agile Alchemy and Agile Odyssey—alongside Rama Krishna Tadepalli (the primary author) and Sayali Sintre—Suchinhita has made significant contributions to the Agile community. These works were published across five countries by ARCCHIE Publications and have received widespread appreciation and recognition on an international scale. Beyond his professional achievements, Suchinhita is a prolific writer of poetry and short stories in Bengali. His literary talents have been showcased at the prestigious International Kolkata Book Fair, with two of his books released in 2023 and 2024. Additionally, one of his poetry collections has earned a distinguished place in the Indian National Library, further highlighting his impact on the literary world. Suchinhita's unique blend of technical expertise, creative expression, and passion for coaching underscores his multifaceted contributions to professional and cultural domains.

ABOUT THE TECHNICAL REVIEWER

Dr. Gaurav Aroraa is a distinguished Microsoft MVP award recipient and an influential Mentor of Change with AIM NITI Aayog, Government of India. He is a business coach with Business Blaster, Government of NCT Delhi, and he contributes significantly to the startup ecosystem. Dr. Aroraa is a lifetime Computer Society of India (CSI) member. He holds certifications as a Scrum Trainer and Coach, ITIL-F, PRINCE-F, and PRINCE-P, showcasing his expertise in project management and IT service management. Dr. Aroraa is an accomplished open-source developer and an active contributor to the Microsoft TechNet community. With a rich background in technology, he has authored books across diverse fields, addressing both emerging and established technologies. His recent achievements include being recognized as a world record holder for his contributions to books in exceptional and cutting-edge technologies. Dr. Aroraa inspires professionals, educators, and students through knowledge-sharing initiatives and mentorship.

PREFACE

As the world transitions into an era dominated by technology—shaping how we work, think, and interact—AI has emerged as the driving force, with the Agile mindset as its strategic partner. This book explores and examines these two powerful paradigms, offering readers a deeper understanding of their complex interplay. The journey begins with a foundation in Artificial Intelligence, tracing its history, evolution, and current state. It provides essential insights into how AI can transform industries and practices on a large scale. We then focus on the Agile mindset and principles, emphasizing core values and methodologies. The book examines the transformative impact of Generative AI within Agile practices and explores AI's influence across healthcare, banking, and transportation sectors. We showcase how AI innovations break boundaries, drive unprecedented efficiencies, and address complex challenges. The book also explores the synergistic relationship between Agile and AI, demonstrating how combining Agile's flexibility and responsiveness with AI's data-driven intelligence amplifies the success of large-scale initiatives.

This book equips readers with strategies to foster Agile thinking in teams and addresses obstacles related to AI project deployment. It provides a comprehensive guide for selecting appropriate AI models using Agile frameworks. Moving into the human aspect of Agile, we explore the impact of AI on team dynamics. We use Tuckman's team development model to illustrate how AI enhances collaboration, optimizes workflows, and transforms interpersonal interactions within Agile teams. We examine AI's role in data-driven innovation within Agile practices, showcasing how AI empowers teams to leverage data for continuous improvement and innovation, from planning to retrospectives. Through the chapters outlined below, this book aims to offer a comprehensive understanding of how AI and Agile intersect, evolve, and redefine industries and team dynamics. It serves as both a guide and a source of inspiration for leaders, practitioners, and innovators seeking to harness the combined potential of AI and Agile. With this endeavor, we embark on a journey to explore, understand, and embrace the boundless opportunities at the intersection of Artificial Intelligence and Agile methodologies.

Let's embark on this journey of learning together.

What's Inside This Book

Chapter 1: Introduction to Artificial Intelligence overviews AI, its history, evolution, and current state.

Chapter 2: Agile Fundamentals and Mindset exploration of the Agile mindset, principles, and key concepts, including the impact of Generative AI on Agile practices and the idea of becoming "Agile.".

Chapter 3: AI Horizons: Innovations Across Industries examines the role of AI in transforming industries such as healthcare, banking, transportation, and more.

Chapter 4: Synergy of AI and Agile: A Primer explores how Agile and AI complement one another in executing large-scale programs.

Chapter 5: Agile Resilience: Conquering AI Implementation Challenges addresses strategies for educating teams on the Agile thought process, highlights deployment challenges for AI projects, and explores key factors influencing AI model selection within Agile frameworks.

Chapter 6: AI Evolution: Redefining Team Dynamics explores AI's impact on Agile teams, focusing on Tuckman's team development model and how AI transforms team dynamics across various stages.

Chapter 7: Data-Driven Innovation: Accelerated shows how AI integration influences critical areas like relative estimations, sprint planning, retrospectives, and sprint demos, highlighting AI's role in shaping Agile team dynamics.

For Whom This Book Is Intended

This book is designed for:

- Agile enthusiasts and practitioners
- Industry professionals and executives
- Academic researchers and students
- AI developers and practitioners
- Leadership teams
- Program/Account managers

Download the source code and colored images:

To download the source code bundle

and the colored images, please follow the link

OR

scan the QR Code

`https://l1nq.com/9788197976858`

Errata

At **ARCCHIE Publications**, we are committed to delivering the highest-quality content in all our publications. We follow best practices to ensure the accuracy of our content to provide our readers with an indulgent reading experience. We believe and understand that our readers are our best judges, and we always use their input and feedback from time to time to improve human errors, if any, that may occur during the publishing processes involved. We invite you to participate in our errata submission process to ensure our books remain accurate and up to date. Please help us reach out to readers who might have difficulties due to unforeseen errors. Please write to us at *errata@arcchieonline.com*.

When submitting errata, please include the following information:

- Book Title
- Reference#
- Author(s)
- Page Number
- Description of the Error
- Suggested Correction (if applicable)

The **ARCCHIE Publications** Family highly appreciates your support, suggestions, and feedback.

Sharing Your Perspective and Providing Feedback

Your perspective is invaluable to us, as it helps us enhance our content and gather your feedback. We warmly welcome all forms of feedback. Please feel free to send us an email at **feedback@ arcchieonline.com**, mentioning the book title in the subject line of your message.

Book Review Invitation

We kindly invite you to share your thoughts. After you've read and engaged with this book, consider leaving a review on the platform where you acquired it. Your impartial feedback can greatly assist potential readers in making informed decisions. Your reviews provide valuable insights for us at **Arcchie**, helping us better understand your perspectives on our products, and they offer authors the chance to appreciate your feedback on their work.

PIRACY

Should you encounter unauthorized reproductions of our publications in any digital format on the internet, we kindly request your assistance in pinpointing their locations or website sources. Please reach out to us at **copyright@arcchieonline.com** and include a link to the infringing material.

If you possess expertise in a particular subject and wish to participate in the creation or contribution to a book, please visit **authors.arcchieonline.com**. We welcome you and assist you to start your authorship journey with **ARCCHIE PUBLICATIONS**.

TABLE OF CONTENTS

Notes   Date:

Chapter 1

Introduction to Artificial Intelligence

Artificial intelligence (AI) refers to replicating human intelligence in machines designed to reason, learn, and take action. It encompasses technologies such as machine learning, natural language processing, computer vision, and robotics, enabling systems to gather information, identify patterns, and perform cognitive tasks. AI is programmed to mimic cognitive abilities, including problem-solving, reasoning, and decision-making, often accomplishing these tasks efficiently in less time. It spans many applications, from automating repetitive tasks to strategic planning and enhancing decision-making.

The proceding image, **Fig. 1.1**, depicts a science fiction-inspired representation of AI. Key types of artificial intelligence (AI) include machine learning, where systems improve through experience; natural language processing, which enables systems to understand and generate human language; computer vision, which interprets data from visual systems; and robotics, which combines AI with the physical aspects of automation. These technologies allow systems to analyze large datasets, identify patterns, generate recommendations, and act quickly and accurately. Consider this hypothetical scenario: You were stranded on a deserted island for 15 years. On your 16th birthday, you return to society and are placed in an apartment equipped with all the modern conveniences and furniture we use daily. Now, assume you haven't been taught what to do or check before leaving the apartment. Suddenly, due to unforeseen circumstances, you must leave while it's raining heavily outside.

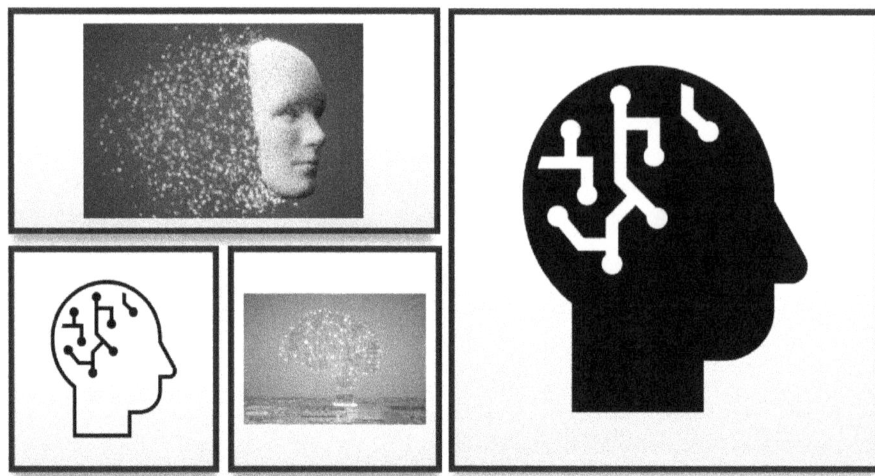

Figure 1.1: *Artificial intelligence*

What are the chances you'll instinctively look for a raincoat or umbrella? Almost none, right? This is because you haven't learned when or how to use an umbrella, nor has anyone shared this knowledge with you. You might even sleep on the dining table simply because no one taught you its intended use. However, if someone showed you how and explained their experiences, your brain would begin learning and adapting.

For example, you'd learn to use an umbrella or raincoat when it rains. Similarly, machines need to be trained with a wealth of knowledge and experience, enabling them to use complex algorithms to perform various tasks or make decisions based on the provided data.

Yes, you're right—by doing this, you are making the machine artificially intelligent. This chapter explores the concept of AI, its history and evolution, its various types, and its significance. The following chapter will delve into the meaning of Agile and the influence of AI on Agile Ways of Working.

The goal of this chapter is to:

- Understand the concept of artificial intelligence.
- Learn about the different types of AI.
- Explore the history and evolution of AI.
- Gain knowledge about machine learning.
- Understand the techniques used in machine learning.

In the upcoming chapters, we will delve into the concept of Agile, examining how AI influences Agile methodologies and how AI-driven approaches impact Agile practices.

Artificial Intelligence (AI) is a branch of computer science focused on developing intelligent machines or systems capable of solving problems typically encountered in the human domain. These processes include learning, reasoning, problem-solving, understanding language, and recognizing patterns. At its core, AI is the study of designing machines to behave in ways essential to human life. Artificial intelligence (AI) is the simulation of human intelligence processes by technology, particularly computer systems.

AI has several subfields, such as machine learning, natural language processing, computer vision, robotics, and expert systems. Before delving into further details, it's essential to explore the origins of artificial intelligence. "Artificial Intelligence" was first coined by American computer scientist John McCarthy. However, the concept of AI predates McCarthy's work and may be profoundly rooted in ancient mythology.
If we trace the origins of AI, we find intriguing parallels in mythology. For instance, in Greek mythology, Hephaestus, the god of craftsmanship, created mechanical servants — early representations of machines performing tasks akin to modern AI. Similarly, in Hindu mythology, Yogis and Asuras are often depicted attaining superpowers through yagnas or divine boons, symbolizing AI's enhanced capabilities, such as processing massive amounts of data, predicting events, and accomplishing tasks with unparalleled speed and accuracy.

These mythological figures often gained their powers through hard work and devotion, like AI systems grow powerful through extensive training on large datasets and iterative learning. However, mythology frequently warns of the dangers of misuse. Just as the powers granted to these figures could backfire, AI's advanced capabilities must be wielded responsibly with a strong ethical framework.

Prometheus, the Greek demigod who gifted fire to humanity, is an allegory for technology's dual nature, including AI. Fire, like AI, represents both creation and destruction — it brings warmth, light, and progress but also holds the potential for devastation. Similarly, Pandora's box, which unleashed chaos and hope, mirrors the dual-sided impact of AI. While AI offers innovative solutions to global problems, it raises critical concerns about data privacy, algorithmic bias, and unethical applications. These ethical considerations must remain central to AI research and innovation.

In Islamic mythology, Jinn — supernatural beings made of smoke and fire — offers another fascinating parallel to AI. Jinn possesses immense power and intelligence, capable of both good and harm, depending on how they are guided or controlled. This reflects the dual potential of AI: it can be a force for innovation and problem-solving or a dangerous tool if misused. These mythological themes emphasize the timeless question of how much autonomy creations should be granted and the importance of establishing professional standards and safeguards.

Thus, the idea of empowering entities with knowledge, abilities, and intelligence dates to ancient times. Mythologies worldwide reflect humanity's enduring fascination with creating intelligent beings, highlighting the promise and perils of such endeavors.

History of Artificial Intelligence

In the modern era, the term "artificial intelligence" was introduced in 1955 by John McCarthy, an American computer scientist and cognitive scientist who made significant contributions to the field. McCarthy, along with Marvin Minsky, Alan Turing, Allen Newell, and Herbert A. Simon, laid the foundation of artificial intelligence. McCarthy's work included research on algorithms, mathematical logic, symbolic AI systems, and the development of the Lisp programming language, all of which established a framework for AI advancement. He remains a pivotal figure in the history of artificial intelligence.

Let's explore the key milestones in AI's evolution:

- **1950**: Alan Turing published the landmark paper "Computing Machinery and Intelligence," proposing the Turing Test. This test evaluated a machine's ability to exhibit human-like intelligence through textual conversations, marking a turning point in AI research.
- **1955-1956**: In 1956, John McCarthy, Marvin Minsky, Claude Shannon, and Nathaniel Rochester organized the Dartmouth Conference. McCarthy first coined the term "artificial intelligence" to describe studies on developing intelligent machines at this event. Herbert A. Simon and Allen Newell developed "The Logic Theorist," the first AI program designed to solve problems like a mathematician. This program demonstrated computers' potential to simulate human intelligence, accelerating AI research.
- **1958**: Frank Rosenblatt introduced perceptrons, a precursor to neural networks. These systems mimicked biological neurons, learning from input data. Although limited in solving complex tasks, perceptrons marked a significant step forward in neural network research.
- **1966**: Joseph Weizenbaum developed ELIZA, the first natural language processor. ELIZA simulated conversations with a Rogerian psychotherapist, demonstrating AI's promise in human-computer interaction and natural language processing.
- **1969**: Shakey the Robot, created by Nils Nilsson and his team at the Stanford Research Institute, became a groundbreaking example of mobile robotics and AI. Shakey used sensors to perceive its environment, create maps, and make

decisions about navigation and interaction.

- **1979**: Hans Moravec developed the Stanford Cart, the first autonomous vehicle with sensors and computer vision capabilities. This achievement laid the groundwork for advancements in autonomous robotics and self-driving cars.
- **1980s**: The rise of expert systems represented a major AI milestone. These programs replicated human decision-making in specific domains using knowledge bases of heuristics and rules, enabling AI to assist in specialized tasks.
- **1997**: IBM's Deep Blue defeated world chess champion Garry Kasparov, showcasing AI's strategic capabilities. By evaluating millions of moves using advanced hardware and algorithms, Deep Blue's victory highlighted AI's growing potential and spurred investment in AI research.
- **2011**: IBM's Watson triumphed over top human champions in the game show Jeopardy! Watson's ability to process vast amounts of unstructured data and generate accurate answers demonstrated AI's advancements in natural language understanding.
- **2012**: Convolutional Neural Networks (CNNs) revolutionized image recognition. AlexNet, a CNN model developed by the University of Toronto, won the ImageNet Challenge, outperforming human experts in facial and image recognition tasks. This breakthrough expanded the applicability of deep learning.
- **2016**: DeepMind's AlphaGo defeated Lee Sedol, a world-class Go player. Combining deep neural networks and reinforcement learning algorithms, AlphaGo showcased AI's ability to master highly strategic and intuitive tasks.
- **2022**: OpenAI's Generative Pretrained Transformer (GPT) set a new standard in natural language processing. Capable of tasks like question answering, summarization, and translation, GPT demonstrated the vast potential of deep learning for diverse applications.

These milestones represent significant achievements that have shaped the evolution of artificial intelligence and its transformative impact across industries.

Evolution of Artificial Intelligence

Artificial Intelligence (AI) is a broad term encompassing all technologies and systems that enable machines to perform tasks requiring human intelligence (**Fig. 1.2**). These tasks include understanding natural languages, recognizing objects or sounds, and solving complex problems.

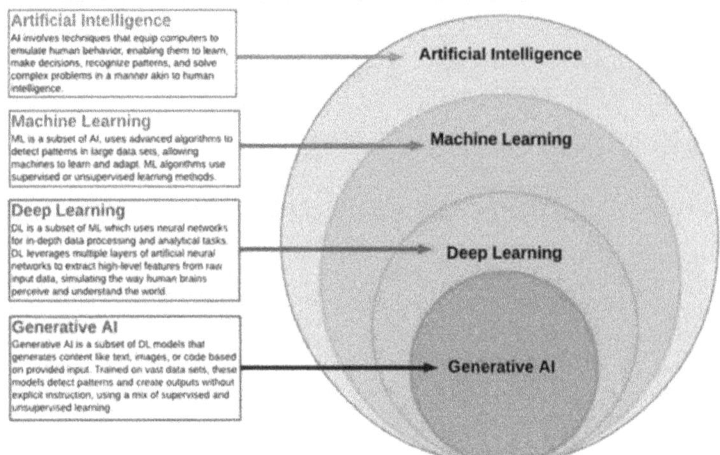

Figure 1.2: *Visualizing how AI, ML, DL, Gen AI are related*

Machine Learning: An Overview

Machine learning is a subset of artificial intelligence focused on developing algorithms and models that enable systems to learn from data. These systems can enhance their performance on specific tasks without being explicitly programmed. The process involves recognizing patterns in input data and applying those patterns to make decisions. Machine learning equips computers to adapt and improve based on their experiences, much like humans do.

Input Data

Input data refers to the information or attributes a machine learning model uses to generate predictions or decisions. These are independent variables or characteristics that describe the samples within a dataset.

Output Labels

In machine learning, each input sample is associated with an output label. This label represents the variable or outcome the model aims to predict based on its algorithms. Using examples and datasets, the model learns specific mappings between input data and output labels.

Techniques in Machine Learning

The primary techniques in machine learning are supervised learning, unsupervised learning, and reinforcement learning.

Supervised Learning

Supervised learning involves training models using labeled data, where each training sample is paired with an output label. The model learns to make decisions based on these specific input-output relationships. Common examples include spam detection and regression applications such as predicting housing prices.

Unsupervised Learning

Unsupervised learning deals with unlabeled data. Without explicit instructions, the algorithm identifies patterns and correlations within the data. Common strategies include clustering and dimensionality reduction. For instance, grouping customers based on purchasing habits is an example of clustering.

Reinforcement Learning

Reinforcement learning involves an agent interacting with an environment to learn decision-making through trial and error. This approach is beneficial in situations where optimal actions are determined incrementally. Examples include robotics, gaming, and self-driving cars.

Machine learning plays a crucial role in enabling intelligent systems. It offers a range of applications across various domains by leveraging structured and unstructured data to generate meaningful insights and predictions.

Deep Learning

Deep learning is a subset of machine learning that utilizes neural networks with multiple layers (deep neural networks) to analyze complex data types. These networks can learn intricate representations and abstractions from large datasets. Deep learning has achieved remarkable success in natural language processing, image analysis, and speech recognition. Machine learning applications span various sectors, including predictive maintenance, financial forecasting, and medical diagnosis. With increasing computational power and the growing availability of data, machine learning applications are expected to expand across a wide range of industries.

Generative AI (Gen AI)

Generative AI, often called Gen AI, represents AI and advanced automation, which can significantly impact and enhance Agile principles in several ways. The upcoming chapter of this book discusses these aspects in detail.

- **Faster Decision-Making**: AI provides timely and accurate analysis, enabling more rapid decision-making. This aligns with the Agile principle of "Responding to Change," as teams can more efficiently adapt to new information or requirements.
- **Enhanced Collaboration**: AI enhances communication and collaboration within Agile teams whenever needed. This mirrors the Agile principle that values individuals and their interactions above processes and tools.
- **Predictive Analytics**: AI can predict project timelines, highlight potential risks, and estimate resource requirements. This supports the Agile principle of working sustainably, minimizing the risk of burnout and overload.
- **Continuous Improvement**: AI can analyze data from past sprints or iterations to refine workflows and behaviors. This aligns with the Agile principle of "Inspect and Adapt at Set Intervals" while emphasizing continuous improvement.
- **Enhanced Testing and Quality Assurance**: AI can streamline testing processes, reduce defect identification time, and improve product quality. This supports the Agile principle of delivering "working software," ensuring each iteration results in a potentially shippable product.
- **Customer-Centric Development**: AI aids in collecting and analyzing customer data to develop products that meet customer needs. This reflects the Agile principle of "Customer Collaboration," focusing on maximizing value delivery to the customer.
- **Efficient Resource Allocation**: AI can identify team members' skills and enable the acquisition of necessary competencies. It supports the Agile principle of "Self-Organizing Teams" by empowering teams to decide how to accomplish their work.
- **Risk Management**: AI helps Agile teams proactively identify and mitigate potential risks, aligning with the Agile "Welcoming Changing Requirements" principle through active risk handling.
- **Personalized Task Assignments**: AI can assess team members' skill sets and assign tasks, accordingly, improving team productivity. This corresponds with the Agile principle of empowering and motivating individuals.
- **Prompt Mastery**: The next section explores the synergy between prompt mastery, Agile, and AI further.
- **Automation of Repetitive Tasks**: AI reduces the burden of mundane tasks, freeing up valuable time for Agile teams. This aligns with the Agile principle of simplicity: "Do the simplest thing that could work," minimizing waste.

While Gen AI supports Agile principles in numerous ways, it is crucial to apply

AI technologies thoughtfully, ensuring that the critical human touchpoints central to Agile remain intact. The emphasis on "individuals and interactions" as a foundational concept of Agile must always be upheld. AI should function as a tool that enhances Agile processes, not as a replacement for the core values and principles that form the foundation of Agile. The detailed impact of AI on Agile teams and processes is further explored in the following chapters.

Different Types of Artificial Intelligence

Artificial intelligence (AI) can be broadly categorized into three major types (**Fig.1.3**) based on approaches and techniques.

Figure 1.3: *Types of AI*

These types are discussed below:

Weak Artificial Intelligence (Narrow AI)

Weak AI, also known as Narrow AI, is designed to perform specific tasks effectively but with limited competence beyond its programmed scope. For instance, when you ask, "Alexa, can you play Beethoven's songs?" Virtual assistants like Alexa and Siri demonstrate the implementation of weak AI. These systems excel at their assigned tasks but lack the versatility of human cognition. Other examples include image recognition systems used by Google or Meta and recommendation engines. While they exhibit expertise in their domains, they do not possess the broader range of intelligence associated with human thought.

Artificial General Intelligence (AGI)

General AI, often called strong AI or artificial general intelligence (AGI), represents the pinnacle of AI development. It aims to build systems capable of replicating the breadth and depth of human intelligence. Unlike Narrow AI, which is confined to specific tasks, AGI aspires to adapt, learn new tasks, solve complex problems, and perform across various domains. AGI systems could demonstrate creativity, empathy, and self-awareness and are not restricted to predefined tasks. Examples include autonomous/self-driving cars and advanced chatbots capable of interacting seamlessly with customers. However, AGI remains an evolving field with significant ongoing research and development.

Artificial Super Intelligence (ASI)

Artificial Super Intelligence (ASI) represents the hypothetical stage where AI surpasses human intelligence across all dimensions—cognitive, creative, emotional, and social. This concept is often depicted in science fiction, such as characters in the "X-Men" or Marvel Universe, where superheroes exhibit extraordinary abilities like flying, superhuman speed, or unmatched problem-solving skills. ASI would match human capabilities and exceed them in ways that redefine our understanding of intelligence. Although ASI remains a theoretical concept, researchers explore its characteristics and potential impact.

Characteristics of Artificial Super Intelligence (ASI)

ASI exhibits cognitive abilities beyond human intelligence, including unmatched problem-solving, creativity, emotional intelligence, processing speed, and self-improvement capabilities. These traits enable ASI to excel in innovation, decision-making, and interpersonal understanding, redefining the limits of intelligence.

- **Superior Cognitive Abilities**: ASI is expected to exhibit superhuman problem-solving, learning, and reasoning capabilities.
- **Creativity**: ASI could surpass human creativity, envisioning innovative solutions and technologies, much like the ingenuity attributed to Iron Man in Marvel stories.
- **Emotional Intelligence**: ASI would likely demonstrate exceptional emotional control and interpersonal skills, far exceeding human emotional intelligence.
- **Processing Speed and Capacity**: With unparalleled computational power, ASI would analyze data, make decisions, and implement solutions faster and

more accurately than humans.

- **Self-improvement**: ASI systems could autonomously refine their algorithms for enhanced accuracy and performance, far outpacing human capabilities.

Potential Benefits of ASI

The potential benefits of Artificial superintelligence (ASI) include groundbreaking advancements in science, medicine, and global problem-solving, enabling faster, more accurate decision-making and innovative solutions to complex challenges. ASI could also drive economic efficiency by optimizing industrial processes and resource management on an unprecedented scale.

- **Advancements in Science and Medicine**: ASI could revolutionize disease treatment, critical surgeries, and astrophysical exploration while addressing complex scientific challenges.
- **Economic Efficiency**: ASI can optimize industrial processes, improve resource management, and enhance productivity.
- **Problem-Solving**: ASI could offer innovative solutions to pressing global issues like climate change and poverty by leveraging its advanced analytical capabilities.

Current State and Future Considerations

As of now, ASI remains largely theoretical, existing mainly in science fiction and academic discussions. While significant advancements have been made in Narrow AI and AGI, ASI is still conceptual. The future of AI holds great promise, with ASI as its ultimate frontier. However, with this potential comes ethical concerns and risks. A world with "fifty Spider-Men and one hundred Iron Men" may sound exciting, but it underscores the need for robust safeguards and governance. Balancing innovation with caution will be crucial to managing the challenges that may accompany the development of ASI. While the benefits are substantial, ensuring ethical and responsible AI development is essential.

Importance of Artificial Intelligence

The importance of artificial intelligence lies in its ability to transform industries by automating processes, enabling data-driven decision-making, and driving innovation. Its integration with Agile practices further enhances adaptability, efficiency, and customer-centric solutions in a rapidly evolving digital landscape.

Agile Mindset and Its Synergy with AI

Agile emphasizes critical aspects such as adaptability, continuous learning, customer-centricity, ongoing value addition, acceptance of change, and empiricism. These principles are vital in addressing today's dynamic market conditions. When combined with artificial intelligence (AI), Agile creates a powerful synergy by enabling teams to derive actionable insights from data and streamline processes more efficiently. Agile prioritizes customer focus, progressive product enhancements, and flexibility in responding to change, while AI's capabilities, such as automation and predictive analytics, align seamlessly with these objectives. Chapters 2 and 4 delve into the interplay between Agile and AI, offering in-depth insights into their collaborative potential.

AI's Transformative Impact Across Industries

AI's influence spans all industries, revolutionizing areas like healthcare diagnostics, customer relations in banking and financial services, IT operations, and logistics through innovations such as intelligent routing for delivery vehicles. These advancements underscore how AI enhances efficiency, accuracy, and innovation across sectors. Chapter 3 thoroughly explores these transformative effects, highlighting how different industries adopt AI to drive growth and innovation.

Challenges in AI Adoption and Agile's Role

While AI presents vast opportunities, its implementation comes with complexities, as suggested by the adage "No pain, no gain." One effective application of the Agile mindset is in breaking down solution development into iterative cycles that address common challenges and involve all stakeholders in decision-making. Agile fosters incremental learning, a crucial element in overcoming obstacles to AI adoption. Strategies for addressing these barriers are comprehensively discussed in Chapter 5, illustrating why an Agile approach is a prerequisite for successful AI implementation.

Enhancing Agile with AI

AI significantly enhances Agile practices by integrating real-time data into decision-making, optimizing Agile events like planning and retrospectives, and refining key performance indicators (KPIs). It also reshapes work practices for Agile roles, providing better tools, interfaces, and solutions for Agile coaches, team leads development teams, and product owners. Chapters 6 and 7 explore these advancements, showcasing how AI improves collaboration, efficiency, and other facets within Agile environments.

Conclusion

This chapter introduces AI's expansive scope, beginning with its definition and historical milestones. It highlights the contributions of pioneers like John McCarthy and Alan Turing and summarizes the key concepts underpinning AI. With a clear understanding of AI's potential to drive human evolution, integrating an Agile mindset can further amplify its impact. The subsequent chapters will dive deeply into Agile principles and demonstrate how an Agile mindset can catalyze unlocking AI's full potential.

Exercise: Test Your Understanding

Answer the following questions and test your understanding of learning from Chapter 1:

Q. 1. What is Artificial Intelligence (AI)?

Q. 2. Who coined the term "Artificial Intelligence"?

Q. 3. What are the different types of Artificial Intelligence?

Q. 4. What is meant by input data and output labels in Machine Learning?

Q. 5. What is Artificial Superintelligence (ASI)?

Notes   Date:

Chapter 2

Agile Fundamentals and Mindset

This chapter will explore our understanding of Agile values, principles, and some related concepts. This approach simplifies the identification of correlations between Agile and AI, which will be discussed in detail in the subsequent chapters of this book. Before delving deeper into the value of Agile, it is essential to understand the reasons behind its emergence. Agile and AI respond effectively to ever-changing market dynamics and meet evolving customer needs. Agile and AI have been developed to address the growing volatility of requirements, a key characteristic of today's dynamic environment. Therefore, 'Being' and 'Doing' Agile and adopting an Agile mindset have become essential in today's VUCA (Volatility, Uncertainty, Complexity, Ambiguity) world and amidst rapidly shifting market trends. These concepts are further elaborated upon in Chapter 4. Agile and AI enhance an organization's ability to respond to change and make decisions based on data-driven insights. Organizations must be agile in their response to new conditions, shifting customer needs, or disruptions in dynamic markets. In real-life scenarios, several companies encountered radical changes during the COVID-19 pandemic. For instance, companies like Spotify leveraged Agile frameworks to effectively adapt to shifts in how people work, especially when such changes created uncertainty in the context of delivering features. AI played a crucial role in identifying growth patterns among audiences, such as the rising popularity of podcasts, and determining where and when resources should be allocated. Similarly, for Zara, the renowned fashion retailer, Agile practices help streamline the supply chain and allow for the rapid modification of designs based on real-time shopper feedback. AI is employed to analyze trends and gain insights into fashion preferences, enabling Zara to provide the right products to the right markets within weeks. By adhering to Agile principles, organizations can enhance their capacity to deliver value, remain competitive, and act promptly in today's ever-evolving landscape. This has led to the emergence of the Agile mindset, driving enterprise transformation.

The goal of this chapter is to:

- To understand agile.
- To understand what you mean by an agile mindset.
- To know in detail about the evolution of the agile mindset.
- To understand an agile manifesto is.
- Understand the meanings of the agile values and principles written in the manifesto.
- To know the summary of the impact of GEN-AI on Agile.
- To understand what you mean by "To Be Truly Agile."

In the first chapter, we explored the definition of AI, its types, evolution, and significance. The relationship between Agile and AI is rooted in their shared emphasis on adaptability, continuous improvement, and delivering value to stakeholders. AI enhances Agile values and principles by accelerating decision-making processes, strengthening communication, and reducing bureaucracy. For example, AI tools can analyze data to identify risks, provide recommendations, and contribute to iterative processes central to Agile, where customer demands, and feedback play a key role. This integration enables teams to focus on value creation, idea generation, and strategic planning while applying AI for detailed, timely, and accurate execution. AI and Agile work in synergy, impacting how coaches, product owners, and team members operate. AI can serve as a tool for Agile coaches to provide insightful analysis of team dynamics and progress, offering specific recommendations. Product owners, for instance, can leverage AI insights to adjust backlogs, prioritize features, and anticipate customer needs. Similarly, AI interventions improve everyday Agile activities like planning, reviewing, and retrospective sessions by providing real-time data analysis, reducing repetitive tasks, and enhancing performance metrics that foster continuous improvement. The core values of Agile, along with KPIs and certain Agile ceremonies that AI manages, ensure a solution fully aligned with Agile principles.
This chapter summarizes understanding of the Agile mindset, values, and principles. Future chapters will elaborate on AI's impact across industries and how Agile works.

Definition of Agile

As defined in English, Agile means "able to move quickly and easily." It is a working method that emphasizes delivering value through small, iterative cycles. Both individuals and organizations focus on strategy, collaboration, and the ability to adapt quickly rather than relying on fixed plans. In Agile, teams work effectively with customers, delivering small increments frequently and using continuous feedback to ensure ongoing adaptation.

Agile Mindset

The Agile Mindset is a way of thinking characterized by flexibility, collaboration, continuous learning, open communication, and delivering value. It fosters an organizational culture that encourages embracing new ideas, welcoming feedback, and striving for ongoing process improvement. For example, instead of following rigid, linear project templates, an R&D team with an Agile mindset would frequently engage with users, identify their needs, and integrate those insights into product development.

Below are the key reasons for the development and evolution of the Agile Mindset, shaped by dynamic market shifts and evolving customer needs:

Increasing Complexity

Over the years, market conditions have become increasingly dynamic and challenging. Traditional project management and product development approaches often fail to manage such complexity effectively. The Agile framework offers multiple methodologies that enable teams to respond to volatile and rapidly changing market conditions tailored to specific contexts.

Accelerated Pace of Change

Globalization and technological advancements have driven rapid change across nearly every market sector. Consumers today demand faster delivery of products and services. Agile adoption allows firms to launch products quickly, enhancing their market agility and responsiveness to consumer expectations.

Customer-Centric Approach

A strong focus on customers has become an essential aspect of modern business practices. Agile development methodologies prioritize customer engagement by involving clients early in development and consistently seeking feedback. This approach ensures products align more closely with consumer demands.

Continuous Improvement

Agile frameworks place significant emphasis on a culture of continuous improvement. Teams can learn from previous iterations and apply necessary changes in subsequent cycles. This iterative feedback loop enables organizations to adapt to changing market conditions, streamline processes, and deliver high-quality products and services.

Flexibility and Adaptability

All Agile methodologies stress flexibility and adaptability. They allow organizations to respond swiftly to changes in market conditions or customer demands, enhancing their ability to seize new opportunities or address emerging challenges effectively.

Collaboration and Empowerment

Through its collaborative approach, agility promotes teamwork and integration. Agile methodologies encourage self-organizing teams, cross-departmental collaboration, and shared accountability for project success. Organizations can foster innovation and creativity by leveraging diverse skill sets within teams.

Risk Mitigation

Traditional processes often require extensive time and resources before client feedback is incorporated, increasing the risk of delivering products that may not meet expectations. Agile frameworks minimize this risk by combining iterative and incremental approaches, allowing for constant validation and adaptation based on client feedback throughout development.

It is important to note that while the Agile Mindset is rooted in the principles of the Agile Manifesto, it has evolved through the experiences and insights of software professionals. Agile emerged as a response to the limitations and constraints of traditional, plan-driven software development methodologies. As we understand it today, the Agile Mindset results from various factors and challenges that shaped its formation and continuous evolution.

Evolution of the Agile Mindset

The evolution of the Agile mindset continues to transform how individuals and organizations approach work and address challenges. Initially conceived as a methodology for software development, Agile has grown into an organizational philosophy emphasizing collaboration, customer-centricity, and adaptability. It encourages teams to adopt short, iterative cycles, collect continuous feedback, and make evidence-based decisions.

Software developers began to shift their approaches upon recognizing that rigid, linear processes often resulted in inefficiencies, delays, and project failures. They explored flexible methodologies to enhance responsiveness to customer demands and improve operational agility.

Iterative and Incremental Methodologies

Agile frameworks like Scrum, Extreme Programming (XP), and Lean Software Development champion iterative and incremental development. These methodologies prioritize creating functional software in manageable cycles, enabling regular stakeholder feedback and iterative improvements. Unlike traditional approaches that aim to deliver a fully realized product in one phase, iterative methodologies break the development process into smaller, more manageable parts. Each phase focuses on providing a functional software segment, allowing teams to gather feedback, adapt to changing requirements, and address uncertainties inherent in complex projects. These methods emphasize collaboration among team members and stakeholders, fostering interaction and continuous improvement. Developers could refine their work based on user feedback, producing better software. Early iterative and incremental practices were pivotal in reshaping software development ideologies.

Collaboration and Cross-Functional Teams

The Agile mindset revolutionized teamwork. Developers, testers, business analysts, and other stakeholders began recognizing the necessity of collaborating on large-scale projects. Transitioning from traditional methodologies, teams embraced the importance of communication, coordination, and active engagement. This shift resulted in more cohesive efforts and improved outcomes.

Lean and Quality-Focused Methodologies

Agile's evolution was significantly influenced by lean manufacturing principles and quality management methodologies like Total Quality Management (TQM). Practices such as Kanban introduced waste reduction, continuous improvement, and a focus on customer value creation, further enhancing Agile's effectiveness.

The Agile Manifesto

The Agile Manifesto marked a milestone in defining and spreading the Agile culture. Developed by a group of like-minded professionals dissatisfied with traditional methodologies, the manifesto outlined values and principles rooted in their collective experiences. While Agile originated in software development, its principles have extended to other domains, including project management, product development, and marketing. Organizations across industries have adopted Agile's values, recognizing their relevance beyond software. Agile continues to evolve as practitioners refine its concepts to suit various contexts and needs.

Agile in Today's World

Agile has become a symbol of innovation, enabling businesses to foster agility and adaptability. Its implementation promotes close collaboration with customers, rapid feedback cycles, and reduced time to market. This approach consistently delivers superior quality and efficiency, resulting in customer satisfaction and business success. The Agile mindset remains dynamic and transformative, reshaping traditional approaches and fostering a culture of flexibility, collaboration, and value-based decision-making.

Manifesto for Agile Software Development

The Agile Manifesto consists of four key values and twelve principles that form the foundation of agile software development. One critical point is that the Agile Manifesto does not suggest that the items on the right side of the values are unnecessary. Instead, it emphasizes placing greater importance on the items mentioned on the left side. To simplify the Agile Manifesto, prioritize the values on the left over those on the right. For example, the second agile value, "working software over comprehensive documentation," does not imply that documentation is unnecessary. Documentation is required to the extent needed, but greater importance and significance are placed on delivering working software that the customer can use. This approach helps the customer, and the team better understand the project's progress.

Agile Values

One of the fundamental values of Agile is prioritizing individuals and their relationships, working solutions over documentation, customer collaboration, and flexibility in processes over rigidity.

The four Agile values are summarized below:
Individuals and interactions over processes and tools: This value emphasizes the importance of people and effective collaboration within a team. It fosters teamwork, communication, and an appreciation that software development is inherently a social process. Visualize it in proceeding **Fig 2.1.**

Figure 2.1: Individuals Over Processes and Tools

Working software over comprehensive documentation: This principle emphasizes that delivering tangible value to consumers by creating functional software should be a primary focus (**Fig 2.2**). While documentation may still be necessary, progress is best measured regarding "user-accessible functionality."

Figure 2.2: Working Software Over Documentation

Customer Collaboration Over Contract Negotiation: This concept emphasizes the importance of involving customers and stakeholders in product development rather than focusing solely on contract formulation (**Fig. 2.3**). Teams that collaborate with clients to understand their requirements and goals can achieve superior outcomes.

Figure 2.3: *Individuals Over Processes and Tools*

Responding to Change Over Following a Project Plan: This value highlights that change is inevitable and that software development should embrace flexibility (**Fig. 2.4**). Agile teams can adapt to new conditions, incorporate requests, and, most importantly, accept change as a constant.

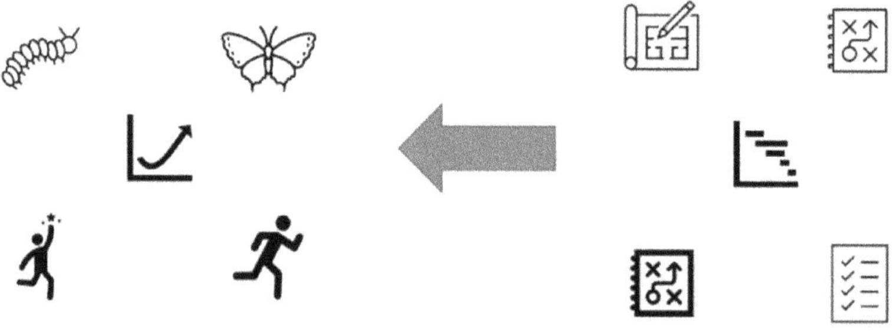

Figure 2.4: *Individuals Over Processes and Tools*

Agile Principles

The twelve principles of the Agile Manifesto provide a comprehensive framework for efficient software development. They discourage adherence to rigid, process-centered approaches by emphasizing customer involvement, flexibility, and incremental progress.

These principles are detailed below:

- Our highest priority is satisfying the customer through early and continuous delivery of valuable software. This guiding principle emphasizes the importance of delivering usable software early and frequently to customers, gathering feedback, and creating value throughout the project lifecycle.
- Welcome changing requirements, even late in development. Agile processes harness change for the customer's competitive advantage. Agile teams embrace change and recognize that specifications are not static. This principle encourages teams to adjust their plans and objectives based on evolving client requirements.
- Deliver working software frequently, from a couple of weeks to a couple of months, with a preference for a shorter timescale. This approach ensures frequent delivery of functional software with minimal intervals between releases, fostering iterative and incremental progress that guarantees continuous value delivery.
- Businesspeople and developers must work together daily throughout the project. Close collaboration between domain experts and developers is critical. Constant communication fosters shared understanding and ensures alignment of goals, ultimately driving project success.
- Build projects around motivated individuals. Please give them the environment and support they need and trust them to do the job. This principle emphasizes creating an environment that motivates individuals and empowers them with the authority and resources to excel in their roles.
- Face-to-face conversation is the most efficient and effective method of conveying information to and within a development team. Direct, in-person communication is preferred for efficiency and clarity. In the post-pandemic era, virtual meetings on platforms like Webex, Teams, or Zoom serve as effective substitutes when face-to-face interactions are not feasible, provided the organization approves these platforms.
- Working software is the primary measure of progress: Progress is measured by delivering functional software that meets user requirements. While documentation is essential, it should only serve necessary purposes, with the primary focus remaining on developing practical, value-driven solutions.
- Agile processes promote sustainable development. Sponsors, developers, and users should be able to maintain a constant pace indefinitely. Agile practices encourage sustainable rhythms of work to prevent burnout and support long-term productivity.
- Continuous attention to technical excellence and good design enhances agility: This principle highlights the importance of technical quality and sound design, fostering adaptability and a strong foundation for future development.
- Simplicity — the art of maximizing the amount of work not done — is essential: Agile teams prioritize important tasks, avoiding unnecessary work to focus on delivering valuable features efficiently.

- The best architectures, requirements, and designs emerge from self-organizing teams: Cross-functional teams collaborate effectively, leveraging their collective expertise to create innovative and efficient solutions.
- At regular intervals, the team reflects on how to become more effective and tunes and adjusts its behavior accordingly. Continuous self-reflection and improvement are key to Agile practices, enabling teams to adapt their processes and enhance productivity.
- The principles of the Agile Manifesto provide a foundation for embracing an Agile mindset, fostering adaptability, collaboration, and value delivery. Organizations aligning with these principles can improve their ability to meet customer needs, adapt to change, and deliver exceptional value.

To Be Truly Agile

Agile requires adopting a mindset emphasizing adaptability, collaboration, and continuous improvement. It goes beyond merely following Agile frameworks by integrating its principles into thought processes and daily practices.

Key elements include:

- Embracing Agile values: Prioritize people and relationships over tools and frameworks, working software over documentation, customer collaboration over contract negotiation, and flexibility over rigid timelines.
- Adapting to change: Treat change as an opportunity for improvement, using it to refine goals and solutions.
- Fostering collaboration and self-organization: Encourage teamwork, trust, and autonomy, enabling teams to make informed decisions.
- Pursuing continuous learning and improvement: Regularly seek feedback and experiment with new ideas to enhance outcomes.
- Focusing on customer value: Deliver valuable solutions early and frequently, incorporating customer feedback throughout the project.

Being Agile involves adopting a mindset that integrates Agile principles into every aspect of work and life, ensuring continuous learning, retrospection, and value-driven outcomes.

Conclusion

Agile embodies constant change, collaboration, and customer focus, addressing the complexities of modern market conditions. Frameworks like Scrum and Lean empower teams to deliver incremental value in cycles, incorporating customer feedback, reducing risks, and enhancing outcomes. Agile Manifesto has transformed how industries approach project management, fostering creativity and adaptability. Future advancements, including the integration of AI, promise to evolve Agile methodologies further, enhancing their impact across industries.

Exercise: Test Your Understanding

Answer the following questions and test your understanding of learning from Chapter 2:

Q. 1. What is agile?

Q. 2. What do you mean by an agile mindset?

Q. 3. What is the Agile Manifesto?

Q. 4. Explain what "To Be Truly Agile" means?

Q. 5. What are the core values of Agile?

Notes   Date:

Chapter 3

AI Horizons Innovations Across Industries

The last two chapters provide an overview of the definition of Artificial Intelligence, its origins, types, and current relevance, followed by the understanding of the Agile mindset, including its values and principles. Before we delve deeper into AI boosting Agile and discover the revolution that Agile is experiencing through AI integration, it is important to understand how AI impacts various industries. AI has profoundly impacted the banking, healthcare, information technology, and transportation industries. By improving facets like banking fraud detection and customer relations, diagnostics and strategic treatment methods, Automation and development of deep IT solutions, and logistical control over auto-mobile transport functions, AI has upleveled the user experience to a state of bliss. Readers need to understand these diverse uses and highlight the centrality of AI across industries before elaborating on the impact of artificial intelligence on Agile practices. Suppose you enter an operation theater and find only robots with surgical instruments. Or let's consider a situation where you only need to sit in front of a machine for any ailment-from minor aches to anything major- and the system will do all the necessary scanning and share a report. Artificial intelligence acted as a catalyst in the technology field and paved the way for the adoption of wonders across healthcare, transportation, banking, and other industry domains. In healthcare, AI has brought unparalleled accuracy in the diagnosis, treatment, and drug trials. It also has extensive involvement in patient care and medical research. Similarly, in the banking domain, AI helped form a new era of financial intelligence and has been used in compliance regulation, security measures, and the creation of personalized banking experiences. AI has applications in transportation and other domains.

To correctly understand the possibility of synergy between AI and Agile, we must examine AI's capabilities across organizations. AI's elements increase precision, reduce or eliminate repetitive work, and contribute to generating personalized value for customers.

The above understanding is a fundamental element for discussing how AI can enhance Agile roles, ceremonies, and practices. In the same way that AI has catalyzed industries to deliver value to the customer dynamically, the combination of Agile and AI expedites teamwork, decision-making, and performance. Whether it is about enhancing the approach for better prediction for iterative planning or about enabling communication with stakeholders via analytics insight, the basic areas of success of AI across industries build the foundation for the future chapters of our book. The future chapters will try to explore the impact of AI on Agile ways of working. Understanding these impacts is essential for the readers to understand why and how AI can foster Agile practices and bring Agile values and principles to make the organizational business value more significant.

Let's look at some of the implications for industries where AI has created landmarks.

The goal of this chapter is to:

- Understanding of the impact of AI on the healthcare industry
- Understanding of the impact of AI on the Banking industry
- Understanding of the impact of AI on the IT industry
- Understanding of the impact of AI on the Transportation industry

Healthcare Industry

The application of artificial intelligence in the healthcare industry has changed the core culture of this sector. AI has already shown a huge impact on accuracy, surgery, medical research, drug trials, etc. Let's explore a few applications where AI aids healthcare, like Diagnostic and Imaging Tools, Early Disease Detection, Genomic Data Analysis, and Clinical Decision Support Systems (CDSS).

Diagnostic and Imaging Tools & Impact of AI on HealthCare

AI has already made an impact on image processing and pathology services. It has improved efficiency and consistency by using predefined algorithms. All these, combined with the machine learning and deep learning approaches, have resulted in better patient outcomes. These algorithms are constantly evolving, with more and more data being fed. Artificial Intelligence & Medical Imaging Analysis Artificial intelligence can enhance the Analysis of medical images in multiple ways. The technologies used in X-rays, CT- scans, MRIs, and ultrasounds capture detailed images within our body.

Below are some of which AI is helping with the Analysis of medical images:

The Diagnosis and Interpretation of Images section below summarizes AI's utility in diagnosing and interpreting images.

- Automated Detection AI-enabled algorithms can detect any abnormalities in the medical images mentioned above. Artificial intelligence is being used to detect breast cancer in mammograms, lung nodules, or hemorrhages in CT scans with higher accuracy than earlier.
- Identifying Boundaries and Segmentation Artificial intelligence can be used to obtain detailed information within medical images. It can segment different organs and tissues, including the tumor boundaries, which has proved crucial during the treatment of oncology.
- Progression AI can be used to quantify the rate, growth, and volume of the health problem over time. This gives a clear and accurate indication of the progression of the disease and the response to treatment.

Improved Consistency the section below summarizes the use of AI in improving Consistency:

- Reduction of Human Error Artificial Intelligence highlights areas of concern in any report that radiologists might overlook. Hence it always reduces the probability of repetition of any error of a similar nature.
- Stability The opinions of different physicians or radiologists might vary on critical or new medical cases. However, if AI is used for the diagnosis and analysis of the images or reports, then the interpretations of the same will never differ, hence providing proper consistency across the entire healthcare domain.

Efficiency the Below section summarizes the use of AI to improve the efficiency of the Analysis of reports

- Quickest Analysis With the help of AI, the Analysis of any reports is completed in the quickest possible time. This is lifesaving in any critical emergency.
- Optimization Based on the severity of the Analysis; AI helps in the prioritization of medical cases. The physicians take up critical cases with priority. This overall process helps to optimize the workflow in the radiology departments, resulting in overall patient care improvement.

Practical Implementation of AI in Medical Imaging The summary of implementation of AI in medical imaging is mentioned below.

- DeepMind created an AI system that can identify more than 50 eye diseases with greater accuracy than expert ophthalmologists. The artificial intelligence system in DeepMind analyzes OCT (optical coherence tomography) and shares accurate results much faster than expert physicians.
- IDx-DR is an AI system that analyzes the images of the retina and confirms if the patient has any signs of diabetic retinopathy and macular edema. This does not require the intervention of any specialists.

Early Disease Detection & Impact of AI on HealthCare

AI helps in the early detection of diseases and hence gives more time to physicians or patients to respond accordingly. The AI models based on machine learning and deep learning techniques are proficient in analyzing huge amounts of data. They can quickly trace the patterns and the connections, which human eyes might easily overlook. The faster turnaround time for the detection of diseases helps the physicians and the patients to act accordingly. The most common examples of predictive models used for this purpose are random forests, logistic regression, support vector machines, and many others. Genomic Data Analysis & Complex Data Processing The entire set of nucleic acid sequences for human beings are encoded as DNA within the twenty-three pairs of chromosomes. This is known as the human genome, and it consists of around 3 billion base pairs. The algorithms used in artificial intelligence systems can process and analyze these data.

- Sequencing of Genomes, the machine learning models can identify mutations related to any specific disease. Artificially intelligent systems can identify the genetic variants from whole genome sequencing data. This in turn results in the most accurate and quickest detection of probabilities of genetic disorder in the patient.
- Transcriptomics and Epigenomics Artificial intelligence can be used to integrate epigenomic data and transcriptomic data for better clarity on the regulation mechanisms of genes. The algorithm in AI detects the changes in genetic expression in the context of its response to different conditions. Hence the systems can identify the markers for many diseases even before the birth of an individual.
- Applications in Oncology Artificial Intelligence have an immense impact in the fields of tumor profiling and precision oncology. AI can process the data related to tumor profiling, identify genetic mutations, protein interactions, and expression patterns, and suggest specific therapies designed to attack genetic mutations driving carcinogenic growth. Hence, AI is helping to form the most accurate personalized treatment plans with higher efficiency and minimal side effects.

Clinical Decision Support Systems (CDSS) & Impact of AI on HealthCare

CDSS provides personalized treatment plans considering specific data like age, gender, and comorbidities. It can assist in the interpretation of medical images and in identifying any sort of abnormality. AI-based systems send alerts for potential drug interactions well in advance. The algorithms used in CDSS ensure proper Analysis of the data from medical images and reports that might be missed by the human brain.

For Example, IBM's Watson has successfully analyzed huge volumes of medical images, reports, and patient data and has provided oncologists with treatment suggestions for cancer patients. The faster processing, accuracy, and personalized patient treatment plan are some of the notable advantages of Watson. Mayo Clinic uses AI-enabled CDSS in the diagnosis of complex medical cases in the areas of cardiology and oncology. Better accuracy, faster detection, optimized treatment strategies, and improved diagnostic precision are some of the main advantages of Mayo Clinic's CDSS.

Robotic Surgery & Impact of AI on HealthCare

Robotic systems can perform minimally invasive surgeries with higher accuracy and control. These are enabled with AI technologies and have the capability of advanced imaging, analytics driven by AI, and real-time feedback for the most appropriate results. The robotic systems can perform complex surgeries through minimal incisions and provide high-definition 3D visualization of surgical sites, enhancing the surgeon's ability to navigate easily to complex anatomy. The enhanced precision also reduces the risk of complications. Since this minimizes the incisions, trauma is also reduced and helps in quicker recovery of the patient.

- **da Vinci Surgical System** is the latest surgical tool in robotics assisted laparoscopic surgical system on the market. Through AI enabled features such as the advanced robotic arms, high-definition 3D visualization and an intuitive console the system allows surgeons to conduct intricate operations with more precision, flexibility and control. The system enhances control over surgical tools to provide the surgeon with precise movements that, in turn, decreases surgical invasiveness, shortens the patient's postoperative healing time, and decreases the likelihood of post-surgical complications. In urology, gynecology, and general surgery the Da Vinci Surgical System is an example of how advanced technical solutions are changing the face of health care for the better by enhancing patient and surgeon performances.
- **Mazor X Stealth Edition** is the next-generation robotic surgical system to improve spine surgeries' accuracy and safety. Building on the principles of artificial intelligence, the integrating system offers precise pre-operative

planning, augmented intra-operative navigation, and enhanced visualization outcomes, which can significantly raise the level of accuracy and controllability in operation. That merger reduces the likelihood of error by enhancing implant positioning and lowering overall surgical risks to benefit the patient. When integrating AI's ability to predict with robotic accuracy, the Mazor X Stealth Edition is revolutionizing spine surgery and pushing the benchmark of surgical excellence.

Banking Sector

Artificial intelligence has led the transformation of the banking sector from its traditional way of working to a new innovative process where it is constantly adding higher customer satisfaction, which is just like the mindset of the Agile ways of working. There has been a phenomenal change in the financial operations of the institutions, customer interactions, risk management, and personalized banking. Let's explore in the next few pages some of the critical areas where AI has revolutionized the transformation in the banking sector (**Fig 3.1**).

Figure 3.1: *Representative image for the Banking Industry*

AI-Enabled Customer Service & Impact on Banking

AI-enabled customer services are quite popular nowadays. Most banks have their own chatbots or virtual assistance. This is giving 24/7 customer support, which was not available earlier. The AI-driven chatbots and virtual assistants provide round-the-clock customer support and help in addressing the customer's issues, hence contributing to enhancing overall customer satisfaction. NLP helps the chatbots to understand and respond to customer queries in the language of their choice. All this assistance and facilitation happens around the clock without any human intervention.

Examples - The AI-enabled intelligent system Erica in Bank of America helps customers with multiple tasks like making payments, discussing financial advice, checking balances, etc.

Many banks use a cognitive virtual agent, Amelia, for managing complex customer queries and improving customer satisfaction.

Personalized Banking Experience & Impact on Banking

Artificially intelligent systems analyze huge amounts of data, which include histories of transactions, patterns of spending, and others, and use the algorithms to provide the most appropriate financial advice for the customers. These systems can track and analyze the trends and the preferences of the customer. After which it uses predictive Analysis to suggest the relevant financial products or actions catering to their needs. This helps the customer get quicker and more accurate advice tailored to their goals.

Examples - The AI-enabled assistance used by HSBC provides personalized financial advice after analyzing the risks and the financial goals of the customer.

Enhancing Operational Efficiency & Impact on Banking

Robotic Process Automation (RPA) automates repetitive tasks through artificial intelligence. This increases operational efficiency and accuracy and allows human employees to focus on more complex tasks or discussions. AI-powered OCR (Optical Character Recognition) systems digitize and analyze documents to retrieve relevant data. This helps with faster document handling for any banking process, along with greater accuracy.

Examples of Operational Efficiency UiPath is an RPA platform that is used to automate back-office processes. It also helps in improving efficiency and in the reduction of operational costs.

Fraud Detection and Risk Management & Impact on Banking

Fraud detection and risk management in the banking sector is one of the most critical areas where AI has proved to be extremely beneficial in providing customer delight. Artificial intelligence technologies can mitigate, detect, and prevent any sort of fraud and manage risks with more accuracy and effectiveness.AI systems adapt over time and analyze real-time transaction data to detect unusual patterns that might indicate fraud in the system. AI can also enhance multi-factor authentication by analyzing multiple factors. In real time, by analyzing the behavior, artificial intelligence uses machine learning to detect and respond to any sort of cyber threat.

Examples Darktrace is an AI-enabled system that uses machine learning to detect and respond to cyber threats in real time. It protects financial institutions from fraud schemes. Kount is an AI-driven fraud prevention platform. It analyzes multiple data points to detect and prevent fraudulent transactions in real time.

Quantitative Trading Strategies & Impact on Banking

Artificial intelligence uses complex algorithms to identify predefined rules and parameters. It analyzes the market data and all the other relevant details and forms trading strategies that capitalize on the market trends only, thus minimizing human emotions and error.

Conclusion

Before concluding, please remember that the impact of AI is magnificent across all sectors. We have shared a few examples in healthcare, banking, and IT. Similar is the impact on transportation, hospitality, and all other sectors. To summarize, we can refer to autonomous vehicles. Autonomous vehicles are probably one of the most remarkable applications of artificial intelligence. The algorithms, machine learning, and computer vision work together to understand and interact with the surroundings. Based on the data collected, they make decisions like algorithms and can proceed on the road without any human intervention. This provides enhanced road safety, reduces traffic, and allows elderly people to travel on their own. Artificial intelligence helps in the optimization of routes based on real-time factors like traffic conditions, road blockage, and weather conditions. Even ride-sharing applications like Lyft and Uber use AI to match the most appropriate drivers according to the passenger. AI helps to know when maintenance is required for the vehicle. This helps in improving reliability and reducing downtime. Traffic management systems use AI to analyze traffic patterns, adjust real-time traffic signals, and detect congestion well in advance. So far, it is quite clear that the main objective of using AI is to increase customer satisfaction, decrease turnaround time, respond to customer queries, and early identify any risks. All these are very closely related to our Agile Values and Principles mentioned in **Chapter 2 Agile Fundamentals and Mindset**.

Exercise: Test Your Understanding

Answer the following questions and test your understanding of learning from Chapter 3:

Q. 1. How has AI revolutionized the healthcare industry?

Q. 2. What is da Vinci Surgical System?

Q. 3. How has AI impacted the personalized banking experience?

Q. 4. How does AI affect operational efficiency in banking?

Notes

Date:

Chapter 4

The Synergy of AI and Agile

Change is the only constant in life. This widely quoted statement resonates deeply in today's rapidly evolving business landscape. In the current VUCA (Volatility, Uncertainty, Complexity, and Ambiguity) world, organizations are compelled to adapt in innovative ways, transitioning from conventional strategies to structured, dynamic approaches to navigate these changes and ensure survival.

- Volatility signifies unpredictable changes or challenges.
- Uncertainty reflects a lack of predictability, where events' causes and effects remain unclear.
- Complexity highlights the intricate interdependencies between objects and processes, adding layers of complication to scenarios.
- Ambiguity indicates a lack of clarity, often due to insufficient or vague information.

One of the key intersections between the Agile Mindset and Artificial Intelligence (AI) is their shared goal of creating resilient frameworks that enable teams to shift away from traditional workflows. Together, they empower organizations to adapt swiftly, meeting the demands of an ever-changing market while enhancing customer satisfaction. The synergy between Agile and AI can potentially revolutionize customer and user experiences, pushing boundaries previously thought unattainable. Businesses can foster improved collaboration and streamline processes by combining Agile's iterative, value-driven approach with AI's data-driven algorithms, trend analysis, gap identification, and feedback integration. This powerful alignment enables rapid adaptation and continuous value delivery, creating transformative outcomes.

In this chapter, we will explore these synergies further and explore how Agile and AI complement each other to drive innovation and growth.

The goal of this chapter is to:

- Understand the synergy between Agile and AI.
- Explore how AI and Agile principles can complement and enhance one another.

Artificial Intelligence Aligned with the Agile Mindset

Although Agile values, principles, and the working culture of Artificial Intelligence (AI) operate in different contexts, they share several fundamental similarities. Recognizing these parallels helps illuminate how Agile and AI can synergize effectively in project management (**Fig. 4.1**).

Below is a detailed explanation of their alignment:

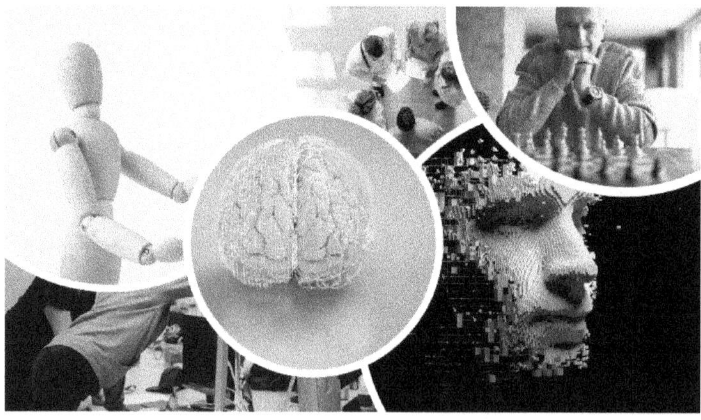

Figure 4.1: *Agile Mindset and Agile*

Operating in a VUCA Environment

Integrated Agile and AI solutions have become essential for organizations striving to succeed in today's VUCA (Volatility, Uncertainty, Complexity, and Ambiguity) environment. Such conditions demand flexibility, data-driven outcomes, and the ability to adapt to rapid changes effectively.

Key Factors and Real-Life Examples

In this section, we will discuss Key Factors with Real-Life examples:

Handling Volatility

Organizations must adapt quickly to changing circumstances in dynamic markets, including shifting consumer preferences and unforeseen disruptions.

Example: During the COVID-19 pandemic, businesses had to pivot overnight. Agile practices enabled firms to adapt to sudden changes, especially in managing global teams. Companies like Microsoft and Slack utilized AI-driven tools to develop features for products such as MS Teams and Slack, addressing immediate market needs swiftly.

Managing Uncertainty

Uncertainty introduces risks and unpredictable scenarios, requiring organizations to learn and adapt rapidly.

Example: Netflix leverages Agile and AI to track evolving viewer preferences. Using iterative development, the company quickly tests new content formats while employing AI models to analyze viewership data and predict shifts in user preferences.

Navigating Complexity

Today's complex challenges often involve multifaceted relationships between causes and solutions, rendering traditional strategies ineffective.

Example: Amazon uses AI to optimize logistics, from delivery scheduling— considering factors like weather and traffic—to customer preference analysis. Agile techniques complement this by streamlining operations, reducing holding costs, and optimizing transactions.

Embracing Ambiguity

Ambiguous situations require organizations to explore options and devise optimal solutions amidst uncertainty.

Example: NASA applies Agile methodologies to design and launch rockets in the unpredictable space industry. AI aids by analyzing vast data sets during test launches and improving designs to enhance safety and reliability.

Augmenting AI with Agile Values and Principles

This section explores the integration of Artificial Intelligence (AI) with Agile values and principles, illustrating how these two transformative paradigms complement each other to enhance team efficiency, adaptability, and overall success.

Agile Values

Let's delve into the core values of Agile and how AI amplifies their impact:

Individuals and Interactions Over Processes and Tools

Agile prioritizes meaningful collaboration among team members, stakeholders, and customers. While processes and tools can facilitate these interactions, they should never overshadow the importance of human connections.

AI's Role

AI tools enhance this value by analyzing collaborative data, identifying sentiment trends, and automating repetitive tasks like summarizing meetings or managing schedules. By taking over mundane tasks, AI enables teams to dedicate more time to impactful discussions and problem-solving.

Working Software Over Comprehensive Documentation

Agile values the delivery of functional software as the primary measure of progress. Although documentation remains relevant, it should serve the context and not hinder the pace of development.

AI's Role

Generative AI tools streamline software development by producing code snippets from simple prompts, expanding them into complete implementations, generating test cases, and automating testing workflows. These capabilities free teams to focus on complex functionalities and innovation, reducing reliance on exhaustive manual documentation.

Customer Collaboration Over Contract Negotiation

Agile fosters ongoing collaboration with customers and stakeholders, reducing misunderstandings and aligning outputs with expectations.

AI's Role

AI-driven analytics tools examine customer feedback, purchase patterns, and browsing behaviors to provide actionable insights. For example, in retail, AI predicts customer preferences, enabling teams to refine their strategies and deliver tailored solutions that align closely with customer needs.

Responding to Change Over Following a Plan

Agile embraces flexibility, focusing on delivering value through iterative improvements and adaptability to changing requirements.

AI's Role

Predictive AI tools such as Google AI and IBM Watson analyze real-time data, trends, and customer interactions, allowing teams to anticipate changes and proactively adjust their strategies. This responsiveness ensures alignment with evolving customer demands and market conditions.

Agile Principles

Building on the values, Agile principles provide actionable guidelines for creating and maintaining adaptive, efficient, and collaborative workflows. Below, we examine these principles alongside AI's contributions:

Adaptability

Agile teams excel in adapting to changing requirements, even late in the development cycle.

AI's Role

AI models detect patterns in requirement changes, provide actionable suggestions, and generate accurate impact assessments. These insights reduce human error and support teams in seamlessly accommodating evolving priorities.

Continuous Improvement

Agile encourages iterative refinement through the Plan-Do-Check-Act (PDCA) cycle.

AI's Role

AI-powered tools analyze retrospective feedback and recurring inefficiencies, offering data-driven recommendations for process optimization. This proactive approach ensures sustained efficiency and quality improvements.

Transparency

Daily collaboration among business and technical teams fosters clarity and trust.

AI's Role

AI tools bridge communication gaps by translating stakeholder requirements into actionable user stories and tasks. This ensures alignment, reduces ambiguity, and strengthens trust within teams.

Technical Excellence

Maintaining high standards in design and quality is fundamental for Agile success.

AI's Role

AI tools like Codacy automatically detect code bugs, highlight design flaws, and propose enhancements. This ensures a robust foundation for software development and facilitates rapid responses to issues.

Simplicity

Agile emphasizes focusing on essential tasks to maximize value delivery and productivity.

AI's Role

AI prioritizes backlog items, automates routine tasks, and aids decision-making, enabling teams to focus on innovative solutions and critical deliverables.

Welcome Change

Agile methodologies thrive on embracing evolving customer needs and market demands.

AI's Role

AI conducts impact analyses to evaluate risks, identify opportunities, and provide insights into shifting trends. This empowers teams to proactively adapt their strategies.

Continuous Delivery

Frequent delivery of functional software ensures early validation and facilitates necessary course corrections.

AI's Role

AI accelerates development cycles by generating code, automating tests, and identifying high-priority features. These capabilities enhance the timeliness and quality of deliverables.

Sustainable Pace

Agile promotes maintaining a consistent and manageable workflow for all team members.

AI's Role

AI automates repetitive tasks, such as data reconciliations and query resolutions, allowing teams to focus on meaningful, complex work. This fosters long-term innovation and improves job satisfaction.

A Case Study on How Agile and AI Promote Customer Centricity at Amazon

Amazon, one of the largest e-commerce companies globally, has consistently prioritized client-oriented strategies. In a rapidly evolving digital commerce environment, Amazon employs Agile methodologies and Artificial Intelligence (AI) to maintain a customer-centric focus. It swiftly addresses customer needs and expectations to deliver an exceptional shopping experience.

Challenge

The inherently fragmented and rapidly evolving nature of the e-commerce industry posed a significant challenge for Amazon. To remain competitive, it became increasingly critical for the company to innovate and diversify the shopping experience while adapting swiftly to market changes. Addressing these demands required prompt and efficient responses.

Agile & AI – A Customer-First Approach

Amazon integrates Agile methodologies with AI to enhance customer satisfaction and optimize delivery processes. Agile fosters structured, iterative changes to meet customer needs quickly, while AI leverages data-driven insights to improve decision-making.

Key benefits include:

- **Delivery Optimization**: AI enhances delivery efficiency by analyzing data for better route planning and customer service.
- **Personalized Shopping Experiences**: Synchronizing mobile apps with Amazon.com transactions allow for timely deliveries, tailored recommendations, and seamless problem resolution.
- **Customer Satisfaction**: These innovations perpetuate Amazon's market dominance and customer loyalty.

Agile Practices

Amazon's Agile practices enable the company to remain flexible and customer focused.

Key practices include:

- **Cross-Functional Teams**: Collaboration between logistics experts and software developers to address real-time supply chain challenges.
- **Adaptability**: Implementing flexible changes, such as same-day delivery during peak seasons.
- **Continuous Improvement**: Streamlining delivery processes to optimize efficiency and reduce costs.
- **Customer-Centric Innovations**: Experimenting with drone-based delivery and incorporating customer feedback.

Artificial Intelligence Applications

AI supports Amazon's operations through:

- **Predictive Models**: AI determines optimal delivery routes and forecasts demand spikes, enabling Agile teams to plan application releases.
- **Enhanced Customer Management**: AI-driven chatbots and machine learning algorithms improve customer service, while human agents leverage AI to expedite complex case resolutions.
- **Personalized Recommendations**: The AI-powered recommendation engine creates highly targeted shopping experiences, driving engagement and satisfaction.

Results: Enhancing Customer-Centricity

Tailored Shopping Experiences: AI facilitates highly personalized recommendations, elevating customer satisfaction.

- **Rapid Feature Deployment**: Agile frameworks allow Amazon to launch features faster than competitors.
- **Improved Customer Management**: AI-driven tools streamline service processes, enhancing efficiency and customer relations.

Impact on the Organization

Customer Satisfaction: Enhanced shopping experiences drive engagement and long-term retention.

- **Revenue Growth**: The synergy between Agile and AI contributes to Amazon's sustained revenue growth and market leadership.
- **Innovation and Leadership**: Rapid development cycles combined with AI insights enable Amazon to lead with innovations like Alexa voice shopping and same-day delivery.

Amazon's Agile culture is deeply embedded in its operations, emphasizing that customer-centricity is key to success. By combining Agile and AI, Amazon remains a flexible, customer-focused market leader.

Generative AI Prompts: Augmenting Agile Roles

This section delves into the transformative potential of Generative AI in supporting Agile values and principles, emphasizing its application within critical Agile roles such as Scrum Masters/Team Coaches and Agile Coaches. By integrating AI-driven insights, these roles can foster greater collaboration, adaptability, and value delivery in Agile teams.

A cornerstone of this exploration is the Prompt Mastery Framework, introduced in Chapter 6: AI Evolution Redefining Team Dynamics. This framework is a structured approach to leveraging AI to enhance Agile practices, ensuring alignment with team goals and stakeholder expectations.

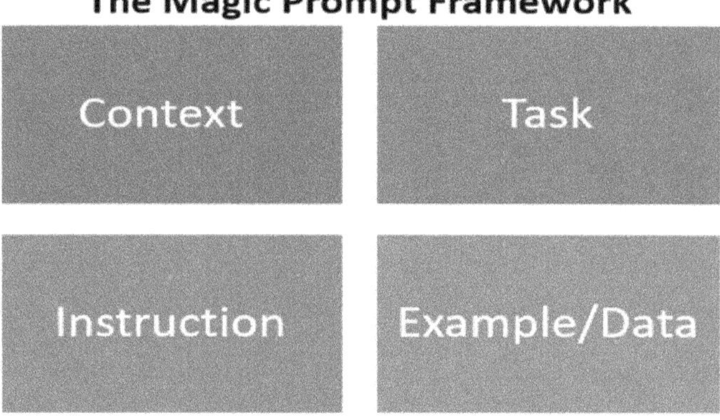

Figure 4.2: The Magic Prompt Framework

Framework

In this section, we will discuss the framework depicted in Fig.4.2:

Strategic Prompt Guidelines

Generative AI can be a powerful ally when utilized with carefully crafted prompts. The framework outlines strategies for creating prompts tailored to specific Agile scenarios, enabling practitioners to extract actionable insights, enhance decision-making, and facilitate team engagement.

For example:

- Prompts designed to identify and prioritize customer-centric user stories.
- Questions that uncover underlying blockers in sprint progress.

Practical Examples

Real-world application of the framework demonstrates AI's potential in key Agile ceremonies and practices, including:

- Backlog Refinement: Crafting prompts to analyze user story clarity, dependencies, and value alignment. AI tools can suggest missing acceptance criteria or highlight potential risks.
- Sprint Planning: Using AI to simulate workload distribution, forecast sprint capacity, and recommend optimal sequencing of tasks to maximize value delivery.
- Retrospective Analysis: Generating insights on recurring patterns in team feedback and suggesting actionable steps to enhance future sprints.

Outcome-Focused Thinking

A pivotal shift in Agile coaching involves steering teams from task-oriented execution toward results-driven outcomes. The framework equips Agile practitioners to use AI for defining success metrics, aligning team efforts with overarching objectives, and fostering a culture of continuous improvement.

For instance:

- Prompting AI to identify the impact of recent changes on key performance indicators (KPIs).
- Leveraging AI-generated scenarios to explore innovative ways of delivering value to end-users.

Expanded Perspective

In addition to the immediate benefits for Scrum Masters and Agile Coaches, integrating AI through the Prompt Mastery Framework has far-reaching implications for Agile organizations. By embracing these techniques:

- Teams can navigate complexities more effectively, leveraging AI to uncover hidden insights and patterns.
- Stakeholders benefit from enhanced transparency, with AI tools providing data-driven progress updates and forecasts.
- Organizations can embed a culture of innovation, encouraging experimentation and learning through AI-enabled feedback loops.

Through thoughtful implementation, Generative AI can act as a catalyst for agility, helping teams and organizations adapt more rapidly to change while staying true to Agile's core values and principles.

Conclusion

The fusion of Agile methodologies with AI technologies offers unparalleled flexibility, efficiency, and innovation in project management. By leveraging the strengths of both, organizations can navigate volatile, uncertain, complex, and ambiguous (VUCA) environments while fostering collaboration and delivering continuous value. This synergy not only equips teams to respond to change but also positions them as leaders in their respective industries.

Exercise: Test Your Understanding

Answer the following questions and test your understanding of learning from Chapter 4:

Q. 1. Is "Continuous Improvement" supported in Agile?

Q. 2. Is documentation unnecessary in Agile projects?

Q. 3. What does "Individuals and Interactions over Processes and Tools" mean?

Q. 4. Fill in the blanks: "Customer Collaboration over ____________________."

Q. 5. How does Agile prioritize collaboration and adaptability over rigid processes?

Chapter 5

Agile Resilience Conquering AI Implementation Challenges

Both Artificial Intelligence (AI) and Agile have taken time to develop and gain widespread adoption. AI has existed since the 1950s, while Lean Agile emerged in the 1980s. Initially, this knowledge was held by experts who conducted numerous experiments to determine its practical commercial applications. For AI, this phase began in the late 1990s when IBM developed the supercomputer Deep Blue. As a result, he was intelligent enough to defeat world chess champion Garry Kasparov. From then, advancements accelerated rapidly, culminating in the Generative AI era by 2022. In the case of Agile, while software development faced challenges with traditional, lengthy phase-gate processes, teams were beginning to adapt to newer iterative approaches. The Scrum Framework was introduced in 1995, but it was not until 2001, with the creation of the Agile Manifesto, that teams understood how to transition to Agile practices effectively. Adoption was gradual, but by 2010, organizations began seeing the benefits and encouraged their software development teams to adopt the new iterative approach. Today, 90% of software development follows Agile methodologies due to its proven success.

In this chapter, we will explore how Agile can facilitate the successful implementation of AI in projects and address some of the challenges AI may present through Agile principles **(Fig 5.1)**.

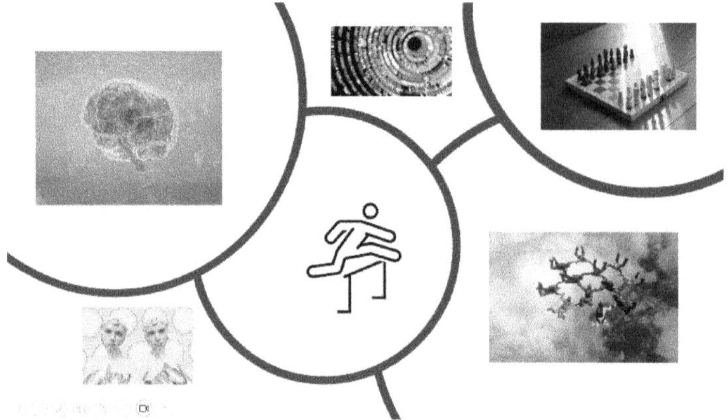

Figure 5.1: *Overcoming the hurdles*

The goal of this chapter is to:

- To educate the teams on adopting an Agile mindset and implementing AI modeling effectively.
- To understand the challenges involved in deploying AI projects.
- To explore key factors influencing AI model selection through Agile practices.

Consider the scenario, Anil and Santosh work for a multinational technology company that develops products using cutting-edge technology. Anil is leading a project for an eCommerce solution that delivers personalized recommendations to users based on their web browsing history. Anil is the Product Manager with AI expertise, while Santosh has recently joined the company as an experienced Agile transformation coach.

In the coming sections, we will explore conversations between Anil and Santosh, focusing on various aspects of their project and how they successfully overcome challenges to deliver an AI-enabled eCommerce product.

AI Education for the Team

Anil arranged a meeting with Santosh to discuss the best approach for their AI-based project, given the team's limited experience with AI.

Anil asked Santosh, "*Santosh, we are building a new eCommerce application with integrated AI features. Our team has a mix of senior members and those with less experience. While technology is new to some, our leadership has directed us to follow an agile approach to delivery. I'd like your input on how we can proceed. We are still in the early stages of finalizing the overall design, and I thought now would be a good time to bring you in to help."*

"Before we continue," Santosh replied, "let's first clarify what exactly you're trying to build.".

Figure 5.2: Learning AI

The image in **Figure 5.2** illustrates the process of learning AI.

"Sure," Anil said. "We are developing an eCommerce application that offers personalized recommendations based on users' browsing patterns. From an architectural standpoint, our application and AI model will be deployed separately on the cloud and integrated via APIs. Additionally, we will need contextual data to train the model. Data security is also a key focus of our project."

"Thank you for the details," Santosh said. "As you mentioned, this is a new application being built by your cross-functional team. What kind of skills do you think they currently have?"

"Good point, Santosh," Anil replied. "I believe they will need some education on AI modeling before we move forward. Additionally, I would request that you regularly coach them on Agile values and principles, which will be very helpful."

"Sure, I'll do that," Santosh replied. "How do you plan to deliver the product?"

"What do you suggest?" Anil asked.

"Following Agile principles, I'd recommend an iterative approach," Santosh replied. "Since you have new team members and this is a new product, starting with a pilot phase with minimal functionality would be beneficial. This will allow you to test the basic AI model and its integration with your eCommerce application."

"This approach offers several key advantages," Santosh continued.

"It will help build your team's skills and capabilities."

"You'll be able to engage stakeholders early as they grow more confident in the AI solution."

"You'll gain insight into your infrastructure needs and how to scale in the future."

"One of your biggest challenges will be data security. This iterative approach will allow you to build up your data, gradually making it more authentic. That does not mean your initial iteration will not provide value."

"Throughout the process, keep your stakeholders aligned and seek regular feedback."

"Great input!" Anil exclaimed. "

Let us begin working together."

Selecting the AI Model

About six weeks into the project, Anil had a conversation with Santosh.

"The pilot was a success! We received a lot of positive feedback and valuable suggestions," Anil said. "We released it to a select group of clients as part of the sampling process. Now, we need to shift our focus to the business aspects. My main challenge is deciding whether to train the model further or use a pre-trained one."

Santosh responded, "Why not hold a retrospective meeting with your team? It's a good opportunity to reflect on what you have learned and weigh the pros and cons of a traditional versus pre-trained model. Involve the team in the decision-making process — it will motivate them and give them a sense of ownership. Of course, you will still guide them and provide input."

Taking Santosh's advice, Anil organized a retrospective session to review the pilot phase results.

During the meeting, the team discussed and identified the following:

Traditional Model

The below table summarizes the pros and cons of the traditional model:

Pros	Cons
Traditional models can be customized to align closely with the project's specific requirements and unique data, providing greater relevance and accuracy.	Building traditional AI models from the ground up involves extensive time for tasks like data collection, preprocessing, model training, and fine-tuning, which can delay project timelines.
Training with internal data helps safeguard sensitive or proprietary information by keeping it within the organization, thereby minimizing privacy and security risks.	Developing such models demands significant computational resources and specialized expertise in AI and machine learning, resulting in higher costs and the need for skilled professionals.

Table 5.1: *Traditional Model Pros-Cons*

Pre-Trained Model

The below table summarizes the pros and cons of the pre-trained model:

Pros	Cons
Pre-trained models can be easily incorporated into applications, speeding up development timelines and aligning seamlessly with Agile's iterative and incremental processes.	Pre-trained models might not meet a project's unique demands and often lack the adaptability needed for specialized applications.
Using pre-trained models can significantly reduce development costs by minimizing the need for extensive computational resources and specialized training effort.	Utilizing these models requires extensive computational resources and expertise in AI and machine learning, which can drive costs and require hiring specialized professionals.

Table 5.2: *Pre-trained Model Pros-Cons*

The Deployment Challenges

Anil and his team adopted the Agile Scrum Framework to build their product incrementally. This approach helped them identify and address challenges, including technical design issues, inaccuracies in the AI model, and UI adjustments using various DevOps deployment strategies. After three months of development, the team felt ready to execute a big-bang release, deploying the product across all target markets simultaneously. To ensure all deployment risks were accounted for, Anil sought the advice of Santosh, an Agile Coach, for a final review. "Santosh," Anil began, "thanks to your guidance, we are now at a stage where we can confidently roll out our solution across all the markets we planned for. Since you have been with us throughout, could you let us know if we've missed anything?"

Santosh replied, "Anil, from a product perspective, you have addressed several critical areas:

- Infrastructure requirements and cost considerations.
- Data management to enhance the AI model.
- Integration of the AI model with your eCommerce application.
- Deployment of monitoring tools to track performance.
- Implementation of robust security measures.

"However," Santosh added, "there is one more step you should take—educating your customers. While your incremental delivery and regular reviews have minimized risks, not all users have been exposed to the product yet. I recommend including a detailed user guide on your application's website as a 'Help' section. This will ensure that customers can use the product effectively and appreciate its value. I am confident this step will leave them delighted with their experience."

Agile Values in Action

This discussion reflects several Agile values that were covered in earlier chapters:

- **Customer Collaboration Over Contract Negotiation**: Continuous stakeholder engagement ensures user needs are met, concerns are addressed, and AI solutions remain relevant.
- **Responding to Change Over Following a Plan**: Flexibility in implementation allows the team to adapt to new insights, technology shifts, and evolving business requirements.
- **Individuals and Interactions Over Processes and Tools**: A collaborative team environment fosters knowledge sharing, joint problem-solving, and the use of diverse expertise.
- **Working Software Over Comprehensive Documentation**: Delivering functional AI models in small increments enables early identification and resolution of potential issues.

Post-Production Assessment and Support

Six months after the product launch, user feedback across all markets was overwhelmingly positive. Business outcomes surpassed expectations, with key performance indicators (KPIs) and objectives (OKRs) showing steady progress.

These achievements, however, did not happen by chance.

As a seasoned product manager, Anil evaluated various analytics tools to understand user behavior and interactions with the application. He explored options such as Google Analytics, Amplitude, and MixPanel, focusing on features that could provide actionable insights:

- **User Behavior Tracking**: Tools tracked user actions like clicks, page views, and events. This data revealed areas where users struggled or lost interest, enabling Anil to create feature requests to improve the user experience. The Agile team prioritized these requests in subsequent sprints.
- **Event Segmentation**: By analyzing specific events and grouping users into segments based on shared criteria, the team could hypothesize new features tailored to segments. These ideas were then validated through A/B experiments.
- **Identifying Areas for Improvement**: Analytics tools highlighted usability and performance issues in high-traffic features. These insights informed improvement goals, which the team addressed in dedicated sprints or releases.

Integrating analytics into their Agile workflow, the team continuously refined the product based on user feedback and validated data. This iterative process ensured that the product met user expectations and enhanced overall satisfaction and success.

Conclusion

This chapter highlights some key challenges in developing AI-enabled eCommerce products and explores how these challenges can be addressed by applying Agile values and principles. It summarizes the advantages and disadvantages of choosing between traditional and pre-trained models. Even during product deployment, there may be obstacles. The chapter discusses ways to overcome these deployment challenges by adopting Agile principles. The next chapter delves into the synergy between Agile and AI.

Exercise: Test Your Understanding

Answer the following questions and test your understanding of learning from Chapter 5:

Q. 1. How did Anil and Santosh decide to deliver the project?

Q. 2. What are the advantages and disadvantages of pre-trained models?

Q. 3. What are the advantages and disadvantages of traditional models?

Q. 4. What key steps did Santosh suggest for Anil? Consider ensuring the product's deployment is successful and user-friendly?

Q. 5. What approach did Anil choose to address the challenge of deciding between using a pre-trained AI model and further training the existing model, as suggested by Santosh?

Chapter 6
AI Evolution Redefining Team Dynamics

The history of the wheel demonstrates how an invention born out of necessity can revolutionize our lives. In the fourth millennium BC, the wheel was invented to aid potters. Over time, the development of high-powered engines has enabled wheels of all shapes and sizes to transform transportation on land, sea, and air, becoming essential in many areas of modern life, including national defense. What used to be a simple legend has become a critical component of our world through advancements in transportation and engineering, promoting swift and efficient travel. The wheel's evolution from an essential tool to a complex machine underscores civilization's progress and the innovation of new technologies. Similarly, AI has reached a new level of significance, becoming a cornerstone of various industries and an indispensable part of contemporary society. Like the wheel, AI's impact spans multiple domains, sectors, and technologies. AI helps Agile teams handle repetitive tasks, analyze data, and find patterns. AI allows the teams to concentrate on more creative and complex problems, leading to better task execution and decision-making with the help of additional data. AI frees teams from mundane activities, offers overlooked insights, and helps them devise more effective solutions in their respective fields. According to Bruce Tuckman's model of team development – forming, storming, norming, performing, and adjourning – AI enhances team dynamics and effectiveness. AI can enhance teamwork in the early forming and storming stages by sharing relevant information and resolving conflicts through quantitative data or task automation. During the norming and performing stages, AI algorithms for real-time analysis and trend identification help teams maintain high performance and adapt strategies effectively. In the adjourning stage, AI can review project outcomes and suggest strategies for future projects. AI fosters overall team growth and optimization by supporting individual components of Agile frameworks.

The goal of this chapter is to:

- To understand how AI impacts teams during different phases of Tuckman's model.
- To explore AI's influence on the roles and responsibilities of a team coach.
- To examine AI's impact on the functioning of a product owner.
- To understand AI's effect on a development team's workflow.

Tuckman's Model & AI

Tuckman's Model, introduced by psychologist Bruce Tuckman in 1965, outlines the stages of team development, which contribute to effective group dynamics. The Model consists of five stages: Forming, Storming, Norming, Performing, and Adjourning. Initially, teams form and establish relationships (Forming). A phase of conflict and competition follows this as members assert their opinions (Storming). As conflicts are resolved, the team establishes norms and works cohesively (Norming). In the Performing stage, the team operates efficiently towards common goals. Finally, the Adjourning stage marks the end of the project and the team's disbanding. Understanding Tuckman's Model is crucial for assessing team health because it provides a framework for identifying challenges and milestones in team development.

Let us explore the characteristics of each phase and how AI facilitates teams during these phases.

Forming: The team is newly formed, and roles and responsibilities are unclear. Members tend to be polite and avoid arguments, eagerly seeking guidance from higher authorities.

- **Onboarding & Team Formation**: Tools like "Talmundo" and "Enboarder" use AI to create personalized onboarding journeys, speeding up the process. AI virtual assistants like Mya and Slackbot guide new members, providing information, answering queries, and helping them settle in quickly.

Storming: Team members are prone to conflicts and tend to resist changes. They feel uncertain and express concerns about the hierarchical structure.

- **Skills & Personality Development**: Tools like "HireVue" use AI to evaluate candidates' skills through video interviews. Neuroscience games can map candidates' cognitive abilities to the most suitable roles and teams.

Norming: The team begins to realize its potential. Although not yet high-performing, things start normalizing as members appreciate each other's strengths and resolve conflicts from earlier stages.

- **Team-Building Activities**: AI-powered tools like "Microsoft Viva" and "Asana" provide personalized recommendations to improve work patterns and productivity. They can analyze work completion rates and suggest ways to improve team interactions. "Humanize" uses Organizational Network Analysis (ONA) to provide data on team collaboration across the organization.

- **Automation of Tasks**: AI can automate routine tasks and meeting assignments. AI assistance can set up recurring meetings, send reminders, and ensure associates respond to emails within SLAs.

Performing: At this stage, the team becomes highly productive. Members operate confidently without supervision, are committed to the team's mission, and focus on problem-solving and achieving goals. Changes in team membership might push the team back to the Forming or Storming stages.

- **Performance**: AI tools like "ClickUp" and "Process Street" optimize workflow and predict potential bottlenecks. They can forecast delays based on past data and current progress and propose reallocations if necessary to meet deadlines.

Adjourning: The team achieves its goals, and the workload is reduced. Management reassigns individual members to other teams, sometimes causing members to feel a sense of loss as the experience concludes.

- **Reflection**: AI-enabled tools like "TeamRetro" and "Confluence" help teams reflect on their work. They identify strengths and areas for improvement and provide recommendations accordingly. Tools like "Notion" create knowledge bases before the team dissolves.

AI & The Role of Agile Coach

Integrating Artificial Intelligence (AI) into daily processes significantly transforms the role of the Agile coach. Here is how AI is influencing work patterns and the tools used by coaches:

Enhanced Decision Making

AI empowers Agile coaches with sophisticated decision-making tools that analyze vast amounts of data, provide insights, and foresee potential issues before they arise. Through predictive analytics and big data, coaches can make well-informed decisions to guide their teams more effectively.

- **Performance Management Insights**: Leveraging big data in organizational settings provides valuable insights into team performance and ways to improve it.
- **Risk Management**: Coaches can be proactive by using AI Algorithms to predict project lifecycle risks. Likewise, AI can foresee organizational risks or strategic challenges, aiding Agile coaches.

Improved Communication

Effective communication is crucial in Agile teams, and AI plays a significant role in enhancing it. AI tools such as chatbots and virtual assistants streamline interactions, provide real-time information, and ensure that team members are constantly updated, allowing coaches to focus on more strategic tasks.

- **Chatbots and AI Assistants**: Coaches can leverage AI features to focus on the project's key points and help the team and organization. AI can answer questions and scenarios proactively for a specific project or organization.

Focus on Coaching & Mentoring

AI allows Agile coaches to dedicate more time to coaching and mentoring by automating routine tasks. Coaches can concentrate on creative problem-solving, skill development, and providing personalized guidance, significantly impacting overall team performance and growth.

- **Creative Problem-Solving**: With AI handling routine tasks, coaches can focus on finding creative solutions, improving individual skills, and mentoring the team.
- **Behavioral Insights**: AI tools observe team behavior, understand current strategies and tools, and identify gaps, helping coaches provide targeted coaching that enhances individual and organizational performance.

Innovation

Innovation is at the heart of Agile methodologies, and AI provides coaches with tools to foster creativity and drive new ideas. By supporting team brainstorming and offering market analysis, AI encourages coaches to explore innovative solutions and implement them successfully.

- **Encouraging Creativity**: Coaches now have more freedom to lead kick-off and conceptualization activities, adopt innovative ideas, and foster new thinking within the team. Tools like "Recipe Pam" can generate innovative solutions based on market analysis and project needs.

Complex Problem-Solving

AI's ability to analyze large datasets and identify patterns enables Agile coaches to tackle complex problems with greater accuracy and confidence. By providing actionable insights, AI supports coaches in devising effective strategies and solutions for intricate challenges.

- **Data Analysis**: AI handles complex problems by collecting large volumes of data, identifying patterns, and providing critical insights, which allows coaches to focus on analyzing data and making strategic decisions with their teams.

Quality Improvement

Continuous improvement is a cornerstone of Agile practices, and AI enhances quality by providing detailed feedback and insights. AI tools help coaches establish feedback loops, monitor progress, and maintain high standards across the team.

- **Retrospective Feedback**: Coaches can now spend more time instilling quality disciplines in the team and establishing feedback loops.

Reducing Time to Market

AI-driven productivity improvements help Agile coaches accelerate project timelines, allowing teams to deliver results more quickly. By streamlining processes and automating routine tasks, AI enables teams to focus on high-impact activities that drive project completion.

- **Increased Productivity**: AI-enhanced productivity enables coaches to identify and eliminate constraints, improve practices, and collaborate effectively to meet project objectives and reduce delivery times.

Automation of Routine Activities

Automation is a critical advantage of AI, allowing Agile coaches to delegate routine activities and focus on strategic initiatives. AI tools manage tasks, schedule meetings, and provide notifications, ensuring smooth team operations and effective project management.

- **Task Management**: Coaches can use AI as their assistant by delegating tasks, e.g., monitoring projects.
- **Meeting Scheduling**: AI tools can also arrange meetings, issue alerts, and suggest the best working times based on team members' availability and habits.

AI Tools for Agile or Team Coaches

Integrating Artificial Intelligence (AI) into project management tools enhances their capability to assist Agile coaches. Various features of AI Tools enhance efficiency, streamline workflows, and provide valuable insights.

AI-Enabled with JIRA

JIRA is a popular project management tool enhanced with AI capabilities. This integration allows JIRA to track work progress and automate routine activities based on historical data and scenarios. Combined with other tools like Confluence, it ensures seamless documentation and improved project management. JIRA's AI capabilities enable it to monitor work progress and automate routine tasks. Analyzing past data can predict potential issues and adjust workflows to keep projects on track. Integration with Confluence allows for auto-generated documentation, making project management more efficient.

Monday.com

Monday.com is a versatile project management tool that leverages AI to enhance task management and boost team productivity. Its various AI features help streamline processes, provide intelligent notifications, allocate tasks, and generate insightful reports.

Monday.com uses AI to make project management more efficient:

- Project Management: AI assists with notifications of project changes, task allocation, and report generation.
- Data Categorization: AI classifies collected data by sentiment and urgency.
- Content Summarization: Outlines extensive information concisely.
- Content Improvement: Checks text quality and suggests improvements.
- Sentiment Detection: Analyzes textual data to offer insights based on sentiment levels.
- Custom Blocks: Uses AI to create unique blocks that fit seamlessly into a website's design.

Conclusion

AI's rise and integration into various fields have greatly benefited roles such as Team Coaches, Product Owners, Developers, and Testers. AI has made a significant impact by automating mundane tasks, aiding in decision-making, improving teamwork, and boosting productivity. Tools like GitHub Copilot and Testim have reduced friction, enabling team members to focus on creative and strategic tasks rather than repetitive routines. This boost in quality, speed, and adaptability is invaluable. However, striking a balance and avoiding over-reliance on AI is essential. Sole dependence on AI can erode critical thinking, creativity, and problem-solving skills—traits essential, especially when managing complex projects. By blending AI's advantages with a human approach, teams can harness AI effectively without losing the unique human touch.

Exercise: Test Your Understanding

Answer the following questions and test your understanding of learning from Chapter 6:

Q. 1. What are the 5 phases of a team in Tuckman's model?

Q. 2. Mention a few AI tools used by Product Owners?

Q. 3. Mention a few AI-enabled tools used by Development Teams?

Q. 4. List five popular prompts used by Team Coaches?

Q. 5. Summarize the impact of AI on Development Team members?

Chapter 7

Data-Driven Innovation Accelerated

As the notion of Agility continues to progress, people have started to turn to a data-driven approach for boosting the team's performance and morale. The application of artificial intelligence has significantly transformed the different areas of Agile practices since AI can now manage massive amounts of data within different systems for decision-making. AI analyzes historical data and defines patterns, which is an advantage for relative estimation. The team can always verify their estimations with the one generated by AI and work if there is any deviation. With the help of AI, it becomes easier to provide relative estimations as it eliminates biases and provides the data required for the estimations. Similarly, AI helps teams predict potential impediments and proper resource utilization during planning, depending on the team's history. Similarly, Artificial Intelligence helps to form more actionable and appropriate objectives while also being helpful when it comes to steady changes in requirements. This chapter explores newer AI applications and Agile trends that provide new dimensions to the future operations of the teams. AI provides opportunities for advanced intelligent retrospectives that provide more reliable insights into collaboration and performance trends. Since more novel usage of AI in review meetings increases the stakeholder's interest, it is safe to state that the future of Agile AI is full of potential. Through exploring these improvements, the chapter opens the discussion of how AI influences the Agile ways of working and can be helpful to the teams dealing with the challenges of the modern software development landscape.

The goal of this chapter is to:

- To understand the Impact of AI on relative estimation
- To know the Impact of AI on backlog grooming and planning sessions.
- To know the Impact of AI on the Iteration demo.

This chapter further explains the integration of AI into critical areas such as relative estimations, planning, retrospectives, and demos to show how the data can influence Agile team dynamics. When it comes to decisions, artificial intelligence tools assist the team in enhancing project efficiency, resulting in faster Turnaround time through complex analysis techniques and predictive analysis.

Impact of AI on Relative Estimation

Artificial Intelligence has brought revolutionary changes in relative estimation and the calculation of the story points. Historical data and metrics are fed into AI tools for more refined effort estimation. For instance, technologies such as Jira's Advanced Roadmaps and Planning Poker applications like "Scrumpoker Online," powered by machine learning, can prompt backlog estimation by using records of earlier iterations to anticipate the time and effort required to execute future tasks. AI in relative estimations reduces any biases during estimation or other calculations, as the results are on empirical justifications. AI tools can analyze vast amounts of data quickly and give forecasts to the team. They consider unique factors like complexities, the team's velocity, and past experiences. With the help of AI tools and data, one can elaborate solutions very quickly and provide the forecast to the team, considering the historical records, the nature of the task, and velocity rates. This capability provides quicker estimation, and a better definition of risks and conditions needed before planning.

AI Tools Supporting Relative Estimation for the Agile Team

This section summarizes three AI tools that help the team during relative estimation.

- Jira's Advanced Roadmaps This tool uses artificial intelligence to help with planning and relative estimation by looking at past project data. It also forecasts how long similar work may take and recommends changes depending on the team's work patterns. This helps define more correct story points and iteration goals based on information rather than human feelings or intuition.
- Function Point Analysis (FPA) Tools, such as QMetry, use Artificial Intelligence to assess the expected effort to perform new Functional Requirements based on the project's historical data. These tools involve algorithms to factorize the estimation of the levels of complexity and story points.
- Planning Poker Apps The current generation of planning poker tools, such as Scrum Poker Cards, uses AI in story point estimation. AI helps in estimation by examining the previous patterns of the estimations and producing recommendations that would be most helpful during the discussions to minimize biases and maximize accuracy.

Advantages of using AI in Relative Estimation

The advantages of using AI in relative estimation are shared below.

- Efficiency Computer-aided estimation tools reduce the project's estimation time and produce results much faster than a human being could ever do. Hence, teams can dedicate their time to strategic thinking and expert work.
- Planning Session Planning meetings can be more effective as AI provides estimates well in advance.
- Consistency AI drives the estimation through data. Hence, story points are more consistent across different projects and iterations.
- Transparency Using AI in relative estimation encourages transparency within the team. AI-based tools analyze algorithms and historical data and give complete clarity on the estimation process.
- Time-saving This saves a lot of time for the team members.
- Empirical Data AI calculates the story points by considering the team members' historical performance and experience.
- Disadvantages of using AI in Relative Estimation The disadvantages of using AI in relative estimation are listed below.
- Data Dependency If the historical data used is correct and relevant, then AI in estimation is effective. Thus, failing to collect accurate data would result in wrong estimates. AI could not understand some aspects of a project or the experience of individuals, which could affect cost estimation and miss some factors that cost estimators consider when estimating effort and costs.
- Lack of human instinct: While we can rely on algorithms to calculate the story points, there can be a lack of human instinct. While doing the relative estimation, the team checks on the most straightforward story and considers that to be the most minor story point. Then, the team members estimate the other stories relative to the smallest one, considering factors like complexities, risks, dependencies, development time, etc. The team needs to discuss if there is any significant disagreement in the estimates by the different team members. Over-reliance on AI for estimation can downplay the team's judgment and experience.
- Anti-pattern Team members feel that they are shifting towards the traditional command-control mode and thus moving away from the conventional agile mindset. Once the estimate is readily available to the team, the team members might not be willing to do a detailed analysis anymore. This might hit back at the Agile team, resulting in spillover or re-estimation of objects after the start of the development.

Like most deep learning algorithms, AI systems rely heavily on the data used during training. Hence, specific project factors or other adversities might be missing. In addition, AI fails to capture the context and make a balanced decision like most team members. One of the shortcomings associated with over-reliance on AI-based tools happens when the model cannot handle new and complicated scenarios. There are factors that require human judgment to estimate. We must understand

and identify those factors. AI validates and fine-tunes such estimates, can provide data-backed suggestions, and can check for inconsistency. AI gives better, quicker, and more accurate estimates. The team's knowledge and perception are equally relevant in providing reliable and more suitable estimates.

Impact of AI on Agile Planning and Backlog Grooming

Planning and backlog grooming are two significant ceremonies conducted by Agile team members. Their proper execution plays a crucial role in the team's adoption of Agile. Planning focuses on setting the pace, tasks, and priorities for the next project iteration, helping the team set its goal. Backlog grooming is an illustrative term, also known as backlog refinement. It helps the user stories meet the DOR [Definition of Ready]. To be precise, backlog grooming is a continuous process of reviewing and prioritizing the product backlog to ensure that product backlog items are well-defined and set the priorities for future iterations. Each of them is crucial to ensure the visibility of the actions taken and the direction forward so that the iterations run smoothly and continuously. AI impacts how planning and backlog grooming are conducted through AI-based tools. For example, Jira's Advanced Roadmaps and Monday.com employ artificial intelligence to help the team plan by predicting the project's completion time.

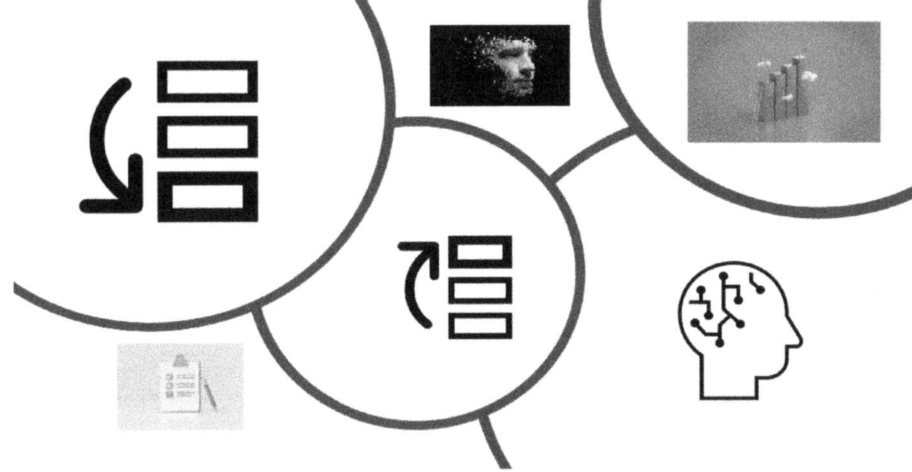

Figure 7.1: *AI Agile Planning*

These tools include features that can assist teams in guessing the duration of a particular task and recommend changes based on performance. In backlog grooming, sophisticated technologies like Pendo and Product board use machine learning to categorize backlog items according to the value of the delivered product backlog items and their complexities. The preceding figure, **Fig 7.1**, represents an imaginary representation of AI, backlog, and planning.

Advantages of using AI in Planning and Backlog Grooming

The advantages of using AI during planning and backlog grooming are as follows:

- **Increased accuracy** the integration of Artificial Intelligence (AI) in planning and backlog grooming has brought more result-oriented improvements. AI tools can leverage past information, estimate the duration of tasks, and rank backlog items better than conventional practices. Teams produce genuine iteration objectives and better backlog optimization than earlier. Below are a few of the tools using AI in this aspect.
- **Jira's Advanced Roadmaps** This AI-enabled tool analyzes historical data and suggests a timebox for any task. The tool identifies which tasks will take longer and, hence, helps the team in the re-estimation process.
- **Monday.com** uses AI algorithms to enable teams to predict the project duration by checking the previously related performance indices and the ongoing project demands. If a team delivered one hundred story points with specific challenges in a previous iteration, then Monday.com can make necessary changes in future estimations depending on those challenges.
- **Product board** This tool uses artificial intelligence to categorize backlog items based on their perceived value and difficulty level relative to the identified user feedback. For instance, if users give feedback showing that a specific feature's availability is important to them, then it is prioritized in the backlog. This ensures that only the most valuable items are prioritized.

If one team is preparing for a new set of user stories to be undertaken, then Jira's Advanced Roadmaps can be used to estimate the effort that is likely to be needed. The team's velocity is 50 story points based on the historical data. An AI-based tool can now guide the team in suggesting whether a new user story with thirteen story points can be planned in the current iteration. Suppose the actual performance of the team differs from this prediction. In that case, Jira AI can modify future estimates based on the collected data, making its estimations more accurate due to real-time information.

However, though AI improves efficiency, Agile teams must supplement such derived information with the proper agile coaching or mentoring factor to avoid methodology-skewed planning and grooming mechanisms by AI information.

- **Efficiency** Using AI during planning and backlog grooming has enhanced efficiency. Most of the routine processes are now automated and provide the necessary information for decision-making. AI tools are used in these processes as they help in computational calculations such as forecast, analysis, and prioritization, freeing up time for the Agile teams to undertake more strategic considerations. Planning becomes more effective. A few examples of the tools in this aspect are as follows.
- **Jira's Advanced Roadmaps** This, being AI, requires no manual input and

adapts to create a comprehensive project roadmap where each iteration is predicted based on past performance. It also alerts the teams of scheduling clashes and enables them to modify plans. For example, Jira can recommend changes in the overall goals by considering the velocity history and current team availability while saving time on planning.

- **Monday.com** is an AI-enabled tool that enables easy scheduling and schedule modification. This tool can anticipate resource requirements and automate task allocation.
- **Product board** in backlog grooming, this tool applies Artificial Intelligence to check and prioritize all user feedback. The product managers can immediately recognize the prioritized tasks and edit the backlog effectively.

For instance, consider a team planning an iteration using "Jira's Advanced Roadmaps." The team estimated that 8 hours a week would be used for this process in previous periods. The integration of AI allows Jira to determine what needs to be done after analyzing the data of the previous iterations. This offers changes in the progress of work in real-time and helps to cut the planning time in half. AI is advantageous in this aspect as it enhances efficiency while requiring team members to apply their experience and judgment to AI suggestions since we cannot conclude how AI concludes the current context.

- **Data-Driven** Insights First, AI applies data analytics to boost planning activities: estimation, prioritization, and automation. Thus, supported by historical data and current project characteristics, AI can generate more precise estimates of a task and the required resources. For prioritization, several factors such as the feedback of users, the level of difficulty of the data, and the Impact of the task on the business are being considered by the AI algorithms to prioritize the items in the backlog properly to ensure top priority to the most important tasks. Also, AI does repetitive work like scheduling and assigning tasks, thus saving time and enabling the planning phase to be handled according to the team's expert opinion. However, this use of data insights and the application of automation not only enhances the efficacy and precision of the planning but also enables teams to adapt to specific changes in the project and enhance their work processes.

Disadvantages of using AI in Planning and Backlog Grooming

Despite the benefits of using AI, there can be some drawbacks, which are as follows. This signifies the importance of human experience and instincts.

- **Resilience on data quality** in situations where the data used is wrong, irrelevant, or partial, the AI's conclusions could be wrong.
- **Lack of contextual understanding** AI can apply general knowledge to some distinct and unique projects and can completely misperceive the team members' interpersonal interactions.
- **Over-reliance on AI** over-reliance on AI in decision-making can often negate human-based orientated instincts, which are equally important while

evaluating a particular scenario or contingency.

AI tools complement the work of Agile Coaches and Team Coaches, who should be free to deliver more work by engaging with the team. This strategy applies AI to ensure the focus is on efficiency without overlooking one of Agile's most critical components, i.e., people.

Impact of AI on Iteration Demo

Artificial Intelligence assists in multiple activities such as presentations, client feedback, and evaluation of customer feedback and has effectively modified the demo format. The integration of AI improves the review's effectiveness, efficiency, and quality.

- **Presentation Delivery** AI can be integrated into demos and presentations, providing tools for creating spontaneous, appealing visual content. For instance, tools like Tome and Beautiful.ai apply artificial intelligence to create diagrams and slides that appeal to the audience because of the data and figures presented. These tools can help prepare demo materials, simplifying the team's work and making the result look professional.
- **Client Feedback Collection** The feedback from the clients can also be gathered using the different survey platforms and feedback management systems. Survey Monkey and **Typeform** are popular tools that can add artificial intelligence to sort feedback effectively. These platforms can take the form of report generation such that for every client-submitted feedback, a report is generated for easy analysis by a given team.
- **Sentiment Analysis** Application performance can also be determined through sentiment. Sentiment analysis is a component of AI during the client's demos. **MonkeyLearn** and **Lexalytics** are some of the tools that use natural language processing (**NLP**) algorithms to determine the sentiment of feedback or comments and tag them as positive, negative, or neutral. This makes it easier for teams to track customer satisfaction levels and realize areas of shortcomings in an organization faster.

Advantages of using AI in Demo

The summary of the benefits of using AI during the demo is listed below.

- **Increased efficiency** AI tools reduce the time needed to prepare presentations and gather feedback, usually provided during demos, taking time from the team. This will enable concentrated effort to work on feedback given and enhance the team's product.
- **Enhanced Accuracy** AI can process vast amounts of feedback and deliver accurate sentiments. This gives a better picture of the client's reaction and preferences. It is an effective way to make data decision-driven and to set the right priorities for any improvement.
- **Consistent** Quality AI tools maintain the quality of the presentation and

automate the feedback analysis so that there are feeble chances of mistakes. With AI tools, the demo appears reasonably well-planned and professional.

Disadvantages of using AI in Demo

Relying on AI completely in the demo can have a few challenges.

- **Over-Reliance** on Automation Although AI can simplify most of the components in demos, social and personal touches with the client may be reduced if all processes are automated. The appropriate use of AI is not without its demerits, which diminish the Impact on personalized communication and understanding of client's needs.
- **Data Quality** Dependence AI tools rely on the quality of the input data they are fed to perform better or worse analyses. This means that if the feedback collected is not random or if the data collected is biased, then the information given by AI might not be of proper quality.
- **Complexity** and Cost Applying and incorporating AI applications to prospective demos may introduce a new layer of complexity and raise the cost. But please remember that this investment helps reassign manpower to other critical areas, thereby improving efficiency.

AI influences the preparation of demos, client feedback gathering, and analysis of their sentiments, hence increasing efficiency, accuracy, and standardization. Sites such as **Tome** and **Beautiful.ai** help simplify presentation creation. **SurveyMonkey** and **Typeform** are used as feedback-collection tools. Technological tools like **MonkeyLearn** and **Lexalytics** can help understand clients' reactions. However, it is critical not to lose the human touch, collaboration, and sentiments; hence, while using AI, care should be taken to the extent and area of its usage.

Conclusion

Therefore, AI in decision-making processes across Agile projects has altered how Agile teams manage relevant estimations. The efficiency of fast data analysis by AI in estimating uncovers bias in decision-making and increases the accuracy of Agile teams' estimates. Implementing these aspects through Artificial Intelligence can more accurately align backlogs for better short-term performance. Managing resources more efficiently with AI-enabled tools helps minimize the time spent on traditional organizing tasks and resources. The chapter concludes by highlighting future AI use cases in Agile, indicating that subsequent applications will further transform the Agile team's work. AI-enabled tools also allow the team to get feedback on its performance as it happens. They can also give solutions by predicting future roadblocks. AI will be extended to many intricate or strategic assignments in the future, such as creating more innovative and flexible processes, identifying dependencies, anticipating velocity, identifying priorities based on market trends, etc.

Exercise: Test Your Understanding

Answer the following questions and test your understanding of learning from Chapter 7:

Q. 1. What AI tools can be used for estimation?

Q. 2. What are the advantages of using AI in relative estimation?

Q. 3. List five popular prompts used by Team Coaches?

Q. 4. What are the advantages of using AI in Planning?

Appendix-A
Answers - Test your understanding

CHAPTER 1

Answers to test your understanding, Chapter 1

Ans.1. AI is a subfield of computer science focused on developing intelligent systems or machines capable of solving complex problems typically handled by humans. These processes include learning, reasoning, problem-solving, language comprehension, and pattern recognition. AI involves studying how machines can mimic behaviors crucial to human life.

Ans.2. The term "artificial intelligence" was coined by American computer scientist and cognitive scientist **John McCarthy** in **1955**.

Ans.3. Artificial intelligence can be broadly categorized into three primary types based on its approaches and capabilities:

- Artificial Narrow Intelligence (ANI) is also called Weak AI or Narrow AI.
- Artificial General Intelligence (AGI) is called Strong AI or General AI.
- Artificial Superintelligence (ASI)

Ans.4. Each of these categories reflects different levels of machine intelligence and capabilities. The relationship between input and output data in AI is outlined as follows:

- **Input Data**: This refers to the information or attributes a machine learning model uses to make predictions or decisions. These are independent variables that describe the samples in the dataset.
- **Output Labels**: In machine learning, each input sample is associated with one output label. This label represents the variable or entity the model predicts based on the applied algorithms. Machine learning algorithms learn mappings from input data to output labels using the provided examples and data.

Ans.5. Artificial Superintelligence (ASI) is a form of AI that surpasses human intelligence across all cognitive, creative, emotional, and social domains. ASI represents the peak of AI research, wherein machines match and exceed the capabilities of even the most brilliant human minds. While this concept remains largely theoretical and has not yet been realized in practice, key features and considerations for ASI continue to be explored.

CHAPTER 2

Answers to test your understanding, Chapter 2

Ans.1. Agile, by definition, means "able to move quickly and easily." It is a working method that focuses on creating value through small, iterative work cycles. Individuals and organizations prioritize strategy, collaboration, and adaptability to change rather than adhering to rigid plans. Participants in the Agile process work in teams, collaborate effectively with customers and deliver frequent, incremental outputs. They maintain a constant feedback loop to ensure continuous improvement and adaptation.

Ans.2. The Agile Mindset is a way of thinking that emphasizes flexibility, learning from others, continuous communication, and delivering value. It fosters an organizational culture that encourages embracing new ideas, welcoming feedback, and striving for process improvements. For example, instead of following rigid, linear project templates, an R&D team with an Agile Mindset would frequently engage with users, identify their needs, and incorporate that feedback into product development.

Ans.3. The Agile Manifesto outlines the core activities of Agile software development. Created by seventeen software specialists in February 2001 to advocate for a more efficient and flexible approach to software development, the manifesto emphasizes the importance of individuals and interactions, working software, customer collaboration, and responding to Change as its primary values.

Ans.4. To truly embrace agility means adopting a specific mindset and approach to work beyond merely using Agile frameworks. It involves continuous learning, embracing Change, and fostering collaboration, enabling ongoing improvement. This includes being receptive to customer feedback, adapting continuously, and prioritizing functional solutions over excessive documentation. It also involves empowering decentralized teams, enhancing their effectiveness, and adhering to a policy of information transparency across the organization. Thus, being Agile is not merely about complying with predefined Agile protocols but about embodying the right mindset and values to achieve superior results, improve customer satisfaction, and thrive in an unpredictable business environment. It requires adopting the Agile Mindset, championing Change, and consistently pursuing value creation to deliver the best possible products and services.

Ans.5. The core values of Agile, as outlined in the Agile Manifesto, are:

- Individuals and Interactions over processes and tools.
- Working Software over comprehensive documentation.
- Customer Collaboration over contract negotiation.
- Responding to Change over following a plan.

CHAPTER 3

Answers to test your understanding, **Chapter 3**

Ans.1. AI has revolutionized healthcare by enabling predictive analytics, improving diagnostics, and enhancing personalized treatment through machine learning algorithms.

Ans.2. The da Vinci Surgical System is a robotic-assisted surgery platform that enables minimally invasive procedures, enhancing precision and reducing recovery time.

Ans.3. AI has improved personalized banking by enabling personalized financial recommendations, predictive analytics for customer behavior, and automated services tailored to individual needs.

Ans.4. AI boosts operational efficiency in banking by automating routine tasks, reducing human error, and enabling real-time data analysis for faster decision-making.

CHAPTER 4

Answers to test your understanding, **Chapter 4**

Ans.1. Yes, continuous improvement is supported in Agile. It is a fundamental principle of the Agile mindset.

Ans.2. Agile values do not imply that documentation is unnecessary. Documentation should be created as needed, but the primary focus in Agile is on delivering working software, which serves as the key measure of progress.

Ans.3. Agile emphasizes collaboration among team members, stakeholders, and customers. Clear and effective communication helps resolve issues and find solutions that might otherwise remain hidden if individuals work in silos. While processes and tools can support collaboration, they should assist rather than replace personal interactions. For example, tools like shared project boards can enhance visibility but cannot substitute the value of direct discussions.

Ans.4. Customer Collaboration over Contract Negotiation.

Ans.5. Agile prioritizes collaboration and adaptability by emphasizing principles such as continuous improvement, effective communication among individuals, and customer collaboration over strict adherence to processes and extensive documentation. This approach ensures that teams can respond to changing requirements, resolve issues collaboratively, and deliver value-driven solutions efficiently.

CHAPTER 5

Answers to test your understanding, **Chapter 5**

Ans.1. They followed Agile values and principles and planned to start with a Minimal Viable Product (MVP).

Ans.2. Please refer to **Table 5.2: Pre-trained Model Pros-Cons.**

Ans.3. Please refer to **Table 5.1: Traditional Model Pros-Cons.**

Ans.4. Santosh recommended that Anil create a detailed user guide or "Help" section on the application's website. This guide would assist customers in understanding and effectively using the product, ensuring a smooth and satisfying user experience—particularly for those not directly involved in the incremental delivery process. By providing clear instructions, Anil could enhance user satisfaction and reduce confusion during the product's deployment.

Ans.5. As Santosh suggested, Anil decided to organize a retrospective session to review the pilot phase results. The purpose of this meeting was to reflect on the lessons learned, evaluate the advantages and disadvantages of using a pre-trained model versus further training the existing model, and involve his team in the decision-making process to ensure shared ownership and motivation.

CHAPTER 6

Answers to test your understanding, **Chapter 6**

Ans.1. Tuckman's model has five phases of a team: Formation, Storming, Norming, Performing, and Adjourning.

Ans.2. Product Owners can use AI tools, including ProdPad, MonkeyLearn, Zendesk, and Power BI.

Ans.3. AI-enabled tools used by Development Teams include Tabnine, GitHub Copilot, SonarQube, Monday.com, and DeepCode.

Ans.4. Five popular prompts used by Team Coaches are:

- Describe a time when you had to facilitate a difficult conversation between team members and how you handled it as a Team Coach.
- Explain how you have fostered collaboration and cross-functional teamwork within your agile team.
- Discuss a situation where you had to adapt your approach as a Team Coach to address changing project requirements or priorities.
- Describe your strategy for managing conflicts or disagreements within the team and ensuring a positive work environment.
- Explain how you have successfully facilitated effective sprint planning and backlog refinement sessions as a Team Coach.

Ans.5. AI transforms Agile Development Teams by fundamentally altering their roles and processes. When combined with AI, tools like Jira manage projects by allocating tasks, predicting delays, and making recommendations based on past data. This helps teams better prioritize, manage timelines, and boost performance. Consequently, team members focus on innovation and decision-making while AI handles routine, analytical tasks. This integration enhances team performance and makes agile practices more flexible and adaptive to changing requirements and market conditions.

CHAPTER 7

Answers to test your understanding, **Chapter 7**

Ans.1. Some tools that use AI in relative estimation are Jira's Advance Roadmaps, QMetry, Scrum Poker Cards, etc.

Ans.2. Please refer to **Section Advantages of using AI in Relative Estimation.**

Ans.3. Do by yourself.

Ans.4. Please refer to **Section Advantages of using AI in Planning and Backlog Grooming.**

JOIN US ON THE
ARCCHIE PUBLICATIONS
DISCORD SERVER

Connect with fellow readers, authors, and enthusiasts to discuss all things related to our publications and the exciting world of AI, programming, and learning. Share your insights, ask questions, and engage in vibrant discussions to expand your knowledge and inspire creativity. Take advantage of this opportunity to be part of a dynamic community dedicated to exploring the frontiers of technology and innovation. Join our Discord Server today and be part of the ARCCHIE Publications community!

https://discord.gg/z26SenmpEt